INDIAN SHIPPING

INDIAN SHIPPING

A HISTORY OF THE SEA-BORNE TRADE AND MARITIME ACTIVITY OF THE INDIANS FROM THE EARLIEST TIMES

RADHAKUMUD MOOKERJI, M.A.

WITH AN

INTRODUCTORY NOTE

BRAJENDRANATH SEAL, M.A., PH.D.

GYAN

Published by

Gyan Publishing House
5, Ansari Road
Daryaganj, New Delhi-110002
Phone: 011-47034999, 9811692060
E-mail: books@gyanbooks.com

Distribution Network
gyanbooks.com
India, USA, Canada, UK, Australia, France

ISBN : 978-81-212-9753-0 (PB)
First Published, 1912

2nd Impression 2023

Printed at: Gyan Press, Delhi.

INDIAN SHIPPING
Author: RADHAKUMUD MOOKERJI

A HISTORY

OF

INDIAN SHIPPING

IN PREPARATION.

1. **"The Empire of Chandra Gupta,"** by the AUTHOR and NARENDRANATH LAW, M.A.
2. **"Data of Indian Economics,"** by the AUTHOR and RADHAKAMAL MOOKERJI, M.A.

INDIAN ADVENTURERS SAILING OUT TO COLONIZE JAVA.
(Reproduced from the Sculptures of Borobudur.)

[*Frontispiece.*

INDIAN SHIPPING

A HISTORY OF THE SEA-BORNE TRADE AND MARITIME ACTIVITY OF THE INDIANS FROM THE EARLIEST TIMES

BY

RADHAKUMUD MOOKERJI, M.A.

Premchand Roychand Scholar, Calcutta University
Hemchandra Basu Mallik Professor of Indian History in the National Council of Education, Bengal

WITH AN

INTRODUCTORY NOTE

BY

BRAJENDRANATH SEAL, M.A., PH.D.

Principal, Maharaja of Cooch Behar's College, India

1912

द्विषो नो विश्वतोमुखाति नावेव पारय ।
स नः सिन्धुमिव नावयाति पर्षाः स्वस्तये ।

" Do Thou Whose countenance is turned to all sides send off our adversaries, as if in a ship to the opposite shore: do Thou convey us in a ship across the sea for our welfare." [*Rig-Veda*, I., 97, 7 *and* 8.]

PREFACE.

About two years ago I submitted a thesis which was approved by the Calcutta University for my Premchand Roychand Studentship. It was subsequently developed into the present work. As indicated by its title, it is an attempt to trace the history of the maritime activity of the Indians in all its forms from the earliest times. It deals with what is undoubtedly one of the most interesting, but at the same time often forgotten, chapters of Indian history. The subject, so far as my information goes, has not been treated systematically by any writer, and has not received by any means the attention it deserves.

This is my excuse for attempting this subject, but the attempt, from its very nature, is beset with difficulties. The field of work is new and almost unexplored, and one has to work at it singlehanded. I have had to depend chiefly on my own resources for the discovery, collection, and arrangement of the materials.

I have indicated fully, both in the Introduction and in the footnotes, all the sources of information I have drawn upon. The evidences used have been both literary and monumental. For the collection of literary evidences I have had to be at great pains in ransacking the vast field of Sanskrit literature as well as Pali (especially the *Jātakas*) throughout which they are scattered, and then in piecing the evidences together. The Sanskrit texts, as well as the Pali, I have studied both in the original and in translations. Besides Sanskrit and Pali, I have been able to gather some very valuable evidences from old Tamil literature with the help of a book by the late Mr. Kanakasabhai Pillay, now unfortunately out of print, called *The Tamils Eighteen Hundred Years Ago*. I have had also to consider and use all the evidences bearing on my subject that are contained in classical literature, made accessible to Indian students by the translations of McCrindle. Old Bengali literature, too, has been laid under contribution in connection with the account of Bengali maritime activity. Further, I have, with the help of translations, found out all the evidences bearing on the history of Indian maritime activity that are furnished by Persian works, most of which have been made accessible through Sir Henry Elliot's History in eight volumes. Lastly, I have had to use the material supplied by such Chinese and Japanese works as are accessible through translations in giving an account of Indian maritime intercourse with the Farther East.

I have had also to study MSS. of unpublished works, both Sanskrit and Bengali, in the original. Much labour was involved in the search for these Sanskrit MSS., especially those which belong to the class of *S'ilpa S'astras*, a good number of which I found in the famous Tanjore Palace Library (containing some 18,000 Sanskrit works), in the Adiyar Library, Madras, and in the possession of some old Indian artists at Kumbakonam. I have also derived from local tradition and old folk-lore some very valuable materials for the history of the once famous port of Gaur, the old capital of Bengal.

Of the MSS. used, those specially noticeable are the *Yuktikalpataru*, and the *Arthaśāstra* of Kautilya which has been recently published. These two important and interesting, but hitherto unknown and unutilized, Sanskrit works have great value as sources of economic history. The former gives an account of ancient Indian shipbuilding, the like of which cannot perhaps be found elsewhere in the entire range of Sanskrit literature, while the latter throws some new light on the economic condition of Maurya India which will, I trust, materially advance our knowledge of that brilliant period of Indian history. I may also refer in this connection to the Sanskrit work *Bodhisattvāvadāna Kalpalatā* of Kshemendra, which is being published under the auspices of the Asiatic Society of Bengal. This work also throws light on some aspects of economic life in the Maurya epoch.

I have also tried to discover and gather all the evidence derivable from archaeology. The many representations of ships and boats, and of scenes of naval activity, that are furnished by old Indian art have been brought together and adduced as evidence indicating Indian maritime enterprise. Some of these representations I have myself discovered in the course of my travels, and these have not, I think, been previously published. To the kindness of some of my artist friends I owe the sketches of several representations of ships and boats that occur in old Indian sculpture and painting, such as those of Ajantā, and also on old Indian coins.

My thanks are due to Messrs. Bejoy Kumar Sarkar and Narendranath Sen Gupta, my old pupils at the Bengal National College, Calcutta, and now students of the Harvard University, U.S.A., for their kind assistance; and also to Mr. Ramananda Chatterji, M.A., editor of the *Modern Review*, for the courtesy of his permission to reprint those portions of my work which appeared in his *Review*. Nor must I omit to express my obligation to my friend Mr. Benoy Kumar Sarkar, M.A., Lecturer, Bengal National College, Calcutta, whose constant help in manifold ways it is alike my pleasure and duty to gratefully acknowledge.

PREFACE

I have also to express my gratitude to the Hon'ble Maharaja Manindrachandra Nandy Bahadur of Cossimbazar, and Dr. Rashbehary Ghose, M.A., D.L., C.S.I., C.I.E., for the generous help they have accorded me in preparing and publishing this work.

RADHAKUMUD MOOKERJI.

BERHAMPORE, MURSHEDABAD,
June, 1910.

AN INTRODUCTORY NOTE

(By Principal BRAJENDRANATH SEAL, M.A., Ph.D.)

PROF. MOOKERJI'S monograph on Indian shipping and maritime activity, from the earliest times to the end of the Moghul period, gives a connected and comprehensive survey of a most fascinating topic of Indian history. The character of the work as a learned and up-to-date compilation from the most authoritative sources, indigenous and foreign, must not be allowed to throw into the background the originality and comprehensiveness of the conception. Here, for the first time, fragmentary and scattered records and evidences are collated and compared in a systematic survey of the entire field; and one broad historical generalization stands out clearly and convincingly, of which all histories of world culture will do well to take note, viz. the central position of India in the Orient world, for well-nigh two thousand years, not merely in a social, a moral, a spiritual, or an artistic reference, but also and equally in respect of colonizing and maritime activity, and of commercial and manufacturing interests. A multitude of facts of special significance also come out vividly, and, in several cases, for the first time, in the author's presentation, e.g. the teeming ports and harbours of India, the harbour and other maritime regulations of the Mauryan epoch, the indigenous shipbuilding craft, the Indian classification of vessels and their build, the paramount part played by indigenous Indian shipping in the expansion of Indian commerce and colonization from the shores of Africa and Madagascar to the farthest reaches of Malaysia and the Eastern Archipelago; the auxiliary character of the foreign intermediaries, whether Greek, Arabian, or Chinese; the sources of India's manufacturing supremacy for a thousand years in her advances in applied chemistry, etc. In establishing these positions, the author, besides availing himself of the archaeological (including architectural and numismatic) as well as other historical evidence, has drawn upon hitherto unpublished manuscripts and other obscure sources. But the signal merit of the survey is that these facts of history are throughout accompanied by their political, social, or economic interpretation, so that the monograph is not a mere chronicle of facts, but a chapter of unwritten culture-history, conceived and executed in a philosophical spirit. The author's style combines lucidity with terseness, compresses a large mass of facts into a small compass, and is equal alike to the enumeration of details and the march and sweep of a rapid historical survey.

One characteristic cannot escape the most casual reader of this volume: Prof. Mookerji takes his materials as he finds them, and does not clip and pare them down, in the name of historical criticism, or handle them after the accredited methods of speculative chronology. By confining himself to settled landmarks, and traversing his ground by rapid strides, proceeding from epoch to epoch, he is able to avoid the quicksands of Indian chronology. As for the critical methods of sifting evidence, there is a great deal of misconception in the air, and it is best to point out that the methods which are imperative in testing an alleged fact or event are highly unsuitable in a review of the formative forces, agencies, movements, of a nation's history as preserved in the storehouse of national tradition. To take an example from the so-called Higher Criticism, to explode the Mosaic authorship is not to explode Moses in culture-history. In fact, whether in Semitic, Chinese, or Indian philology, the destructive (and explosive) criticism of the seventies and eighties of the last century is now itself exploded, and has been followed by a finer and more accurate sense of historic origins and national evolutions. For the rest, it must be recognized that, while accuracy and scientific criticism, in the measure in which they are attainable in the social sciences, must always be essential to a right historical method, a first sketch or mapping of an entire province, the work of scouts, pioneers and conquerors, cannot usefully employ the methods of a trigonometrical or a cadastral survey.

BRAJENDRANATH SEAL.

CONTENTS.

BOOK II.—MAHOMEDAN PERIOD.

ILLUSTRATIONS.

LIST OF AUTHORITIES CONSULTED.

Abulfeda.—Reinaud.
Account of Shihab-ud-dīn Talish in MS. Bodleian 589.
Al-Bilāduri.
Al-Biruni.
Al-Idrisi.
Anabasis.
Analysis of the Finances of Bengal (Fifth Report).—Grant.
Ancient Egyptians.—Wilkinson.
Ancient India as Described in Classical Literature.—McCrindle.
Ancient Ships.—Torr.
Anecdota Oxoniensis.
Archaeological Survey of India (New Imperial Series) xv.
Arthaśāstra.—Kautilya.
Asiatic Nations (Bohn's edition).
Asoka Rock Edicts, II. and XIII.
Assam District Gazetteer, II.
Ayeen-i-Akbari.—Abul-Fazl.

Bhikshuni Nidāna.
Bhilsa Topes, The.—Cunningham.
Bible, The.
    Book of Ezekiel.
    ——— Genesis.
    ——— Kings.
    ——— Proverbs.
Bodhisattvāvadāna Kalpalatā.—Kshemendra.
Bombay Gazetteer.
Bombay Times (1839).

LIST OF AUTHORITIES

Buddhist India.—Rhys Davids.
Buddhist Records of the Western World.—Beal.

Catalogue of Sanskrit Manuscripts.—Aufrecht.
Cathay and the Way Thither.—Yule.
Chach-nāma.
Chemical Theories of the Hindus.—Dr. Brajendranath Seal.
Chilappathikaram.
Chinese Buddhism.—Edkins.
Christian Topography.—Cosmas.
Chu-Fan-Chih.—Chao Jukua.
Coins of Southern India.—Sir W. Elliot.
Commerce of the Ancients.—Dr. Vincent.
Considerations on the Affairs of India.—Lt.-Col. Walker.
Curtius.

Daśakumaracharita.—Dandin.
Das alte Indien.
De Coutto.
De Vita Constant.
Dharma Sutra.
——— Baudhāyana.
——— Gautama.
Diodorus Siculus.
Disquisitions concerning Ancient India.—Robertson.

Early History of the Deccan.—Bhandarkar.
——————— India.—Vincent Smith.
Early Records of British India.—J. T. Wheeler.
Economic Review.
Edicts of Asoka.—V. Smith.
Epigraphia Indica, vol. iv. (1896–97).
Epitome of Roman History.—Florus.
Erukkaddur-Thayan-Kannanar-Akam.

Fathiyyah-i-Ibriyyah (Blochmann's translation).
Foe-koue-ki.
Fragments.—Orme.

LIST OF AUTHORITIES

Geographical Account of Countries round the Bay of Bengal, A.—Thomas Bowrey. (Hakluyt Society publication.)

Geography.—Ptolemy.

Georgics.—Virgil.

Ghatakakārikā.

Grammar of the Dravidian Languages.—Dr. Caldwell.

Growth and Vicissitudes of Commerce.—Dr. Yeats.

Gujarat.—Bayley.

Gujarat.—Bird.

Herodotus.

Hist. Anc. Orient (English edition).

History.—Orosius.

History of Bengali Literature.—Dinesh Chander Sen.

——— Burma.—Sir A. Phayre.

——— India.—Elphinstone.

——— India.—Sir H. Elliot.

——— Indian Navy.—Lt.-Col. C. R. Low.

——— Java.—Raffles.

——— Konkan.

——— Mahrattas.—Duff.

——— Pegu.—Phayre.

——— Plants.—Theophrastus.

——— Puri.—Brojokishore Ghosh.

Hist. Rome.—Dion Cassius.

Hitopadēśa.

Huang-hua-hsi-ta-chi.—Chia-Tau.

Ideals of the East.—Okakura.

Imperial Gazetteer (New Edition), vol. ii.

Ind. Alt., vol. ii.

India and the Navy.—Sir C. Bridge.

India in the Fifteenth Century. (Hakluyt Society publication.)

Indian Antiquary.

——— Architecture.—Fergusson.

——— Literature.—Weber.

——— Sculpture and Painting.—E. B. Havell.

Indika.—Ctesias (McCrindle's translation).

Industrial Competition of Asia.—C. Daniell.

LIST OF AUTHORITIES

I-Tsing.—Taka-kusu.

Jātakas (Cowell's Cambridge Edition).
——— Ajanna.
——— Baveru.
——— Bhojajanuya.
——— Janaka.
——— Kundaka-Kucchi-Sindhava.
——— Mahājanaka.
——— Samudda-Vanija.
——— Sāṅkha.
——— Suhanu.
——— Supparaka.
——— Sussondi.
——— Tandulanali.
——— Vālahassa.
Journal Asiatique.
——— of the Asiatic Society of Bengal.
——— ——— Baṅgīya Sāhitya Parishat.
——— ——— Bombay Branch of the Royal Asiatic Society.
——— ——— Indo-Japanese Association.
——— ——— Royal Asiatic Society.

Kalinga Huparani.
Kathāsarit Sāgara.—Somadeva.
Kavikankan Chandi.
Koch Bihar and Assam.—Blochmann.
Kwai-Yuen Catalogue of the Chinese Tripitaka.

Les Hindous.—F. Baltazar Solvyns.
Life in Ancient India.—Mrs. Spier.
Life of Godama.—Bishop Bigandet.

Madras Review (1902).
Mahābhārata.
——— ——— Adi parva.
——— ——— Karṇa parva.
——— ——— Śānti parva.
——— ——— Savā parva.

Mahāwaṅso.—Turnour.

Mal Fuzat-i-Timuri.

Manasāmaṅgala (an old Bengali manuscript).—Jagajiban.

Manual of Buddhism.—Hardy.

Mémoires.—Reinaud.

Mission Life.

MS. Bodleian 598 (translated by Mr. Jadunath Sarkar).

Mullaipaddu.

Natural History.—Pliny.

Nihon-ko-ki.

Nītiśataka.—Vartṛihari.

Notices of Sanskrit Manuscripts, vol. i.

Numismata Orientalia.—Sir Walter Elliot.

Oaranara-Puram.

Old Bengali Manuscripts.

Origin and Growth of Religion among the Babylonians.—Dr. Sayce's Hibbert Lectures, 1887.

Origin of the Indian Brahma Alphabet.—Bühler.

Orissa.—Hunter.

Paddinappalai.

Paintings in the Buddhist Cave-Temples of Ajanta.—Griffiths.

Pañchasiddhāntikā.

Papers relating to Shipping in India.—Phipps.

Parthia.—Rawlinson.

Periplus of the Erythraean Sea.

Pitakas.

—— Aṅguttara.

—— Digha Nikaya.

—— Saṅyutta Nikaya.

—— Sutta.

—— Vinaya.

Portuguese Asia.—Stevenson.

Portuguese in India.—Danvers.

Protāpāditya.—Nikhilnath Roy.

Provinces of the Roman Empire.—Mommsen.
Purāṇas.
——— Bhāgavata.
——— Garuḍa.
——— Mārkaṇdeya.
——— Padma.
——— Varāha.
——— Vāyu.

Raghuvaṁsam.—Kālidāsa.
Rāja-Taraṅgini.
Rājāvalliya.
Rāmāyaṇa.
——— Ayodhyā kāndam.
——— Kiskindhyā kāndam.
Ratnāvalī.—King Harsha.
Register of Ships Built on the Hugli.
Report on the Old Records of the India Office.—Birdwood
Ṛig-Veda.
Rise of the Portuguese Power in India.—Whiteway.
Roman Empire.—Gibbon.
Ruijukokushi.

Sacred Books of Ceylon.—Upham.
Sakuntalā.—Kālidāsa.
Saṁhitā.
——— Manu.
——— Vrihat.
——— Yājñavalkya.
Sanchi and its Remains.—Maisley.
Śiśupālabadha.—Magh.
Si-yu-ki.
Spectator.
Statistical Account of Bengal.—Hunter.
Strabo.
Sungshih.
Suyshoo.
Takmilla-i-Akbar-nāma.

LIST OF AUTHORITIES

Tamils Eighteen Hundred Years Ago, The.—V. K. Pillay.
Tarikh-i-Firozshahi.—Burni.
Tarikh-i-Masumi.
Technical History of Commerce.—Dr. Yeats.
Thirty Years in India.—Major Bevan.
Topography of Dacca.—Taylor.
Travels of De Barros.
——— Hiuen Tsang.
——— Marco Polo (Marsden's translation).
——— Varthema.—Badger.

Voyages.—Kerr, edited by Stevenson.
Vṛiksha-Āyurveda.

Wassaf.
Western Origin of Chinese Civilization.

Yātrātattva.—Raghunandan.
Yuktikalpataru (manuscript).

Z. D. M. G.

INDIAN SHIPPING.

INTRODUCTION.

I.—Isolation and Intercourse.

Even a superficial view of the physical features of India cannot fail to show that there is hardly any part of the world better marked out by nature as a region by itself than India. It is a region, indeed, full of contrasts in physical features and climate, but the features that divide and isolate it as a whole from surrounding regions are too clear to be overlooked. In truth, the whole of India, in spite of assertions to the contrary made by some geographers, is easily perceived to be a single country endowed with a sharply defined individuality, and beneath her truly manifold and bewildering variety there is a fundamental geographical unity, a complete territorial synthesis.

Mountain-guarded and sea-girt as she is on the north and the south, India looks as if she had been meant by nature to remain aloof from the rest of the world and to develop her civilization in isolation, untouched by the currents that stir humanity abroad. And yet there is hardly any country in the world that presents such an eventful record of intercourse with foreign countries. The geography of India points to her natural isolation; but the history of India reveals other facts. And if we study that history carefully from the earliest times we shall easily recognize that contact or intercourse with other countries has been a no less potent factor in its making than isolation. It has been well said that none of the greatest movements in the world which have influenced the history of mankind have failed to touch India and contribute to the development and richness of her extraordinarily varied culture and civilization. Above all comprehension and beyond all human insight is that mysterious impulse which gave birth to the momentous movement of Aryan migration and expansion, so big with consequences, and by far the most important event in the world's history. And it is a commonplace of history that one of the main streams of this great migration of the pioneers of the world's civilization entered India through her north-western mountain passes to build up her spiritual character, even as the Indus and the Ganges have broken through the Himālayas to create her physical character. For centuries these Indo-Aryans pushed on their work of colonizing India amid struggles and conflicts with the original inhabitants of the country, and developed a civilization that is reflected in the literature they have created. Then rose Buddhism, the first of world-religions, a product of the Indian soil which extended its influence beyond its limits over all countries lying east and north of India—from the steppes of the Mongols and the mountainous wildernesses of Tibet, through Japan, and on the south and east far into the Indian Archipelago. For centuries India stood out as the heart of the Old World, moulding and dominating its thought and life. Meanwhile there continued to beat upon Indian shores successive waves of foreign influence, such as the Iranian influence flowing from the first veritable empire of the ancient Orient, the empire of the Achaemenides, which under Darius included within itself the whole of Sindh and a considerable portion of the Punjab east of the Indus, forming his twentieth satrapy and yielding the enormous tribute of fully a million sterling, an influence that left some marks upon Indian art and architecture and methods of government and administration; the Hellenic influence beginning from Alexander's invasion and exercised by a succession of Greek rulers of the Punjab and neighbouring regions, but "which touched only the fringe of Indian civilization"; and the Graeco-Roman influence during the time of the Kushan or Indo-Scythian kings. Then, also, the two great civilizing forces of the world that next arose did not fail to touch India and contribute to her making, viz. the Islamic culture and civilization, and the European, which, following in the wake of foreign invasions and commerce, has continued to influence Indian thought and life to this day. India, therefore, is a favoured country where all the diversities of human culture have met to build up an extraordinarily rich and synthetic culture. Thus intercourse is as much a characteristic of the history of India as isolation.

Hardly less convincing than these facts of the political intercourse of India are the facts of her commercial intercourse with foreign countries with which we are more directly concerned. We shall have ample evidence to show that for full thirty centuries India stood out as the very heart of the Old World, and maintained her position as one of the foremost maritime countries. She had colonies in Pegu, in Cambodia, in Java, in Sumatra, in Borneo, and even in the countries of the Farther East as far as Japan. She had trading settlements in Southern China, in the Malayan peninsula, in Arabia, and in all the chief cities of Persia and all over the east coast of Africa. She cultivated trade relations not only with the countries of Asia, but also with the whole of the then known world, including the countries under the dominion of the Roman Empire, and both the East and the West became the theatre of Indian commercial activity and gave scope to her naval energy and throbbing international life.

It will thus be seen that instead of the rigid isolation apparently decreed to her by nature, we find a remarkably active intercourse with foreign countries established by the efforts of man, and a conquest achieved over the natural environment. The great and almost impregnable barriers on the north are pierced by mountain-passes which have been throughout used as the pathways of commerce and communication with the external world. Towards the south the ocean from its very nature proved a far more effective and fatal barrier to the cultivation of foreign relations, till the rapid development of national shipping triumphed over that obstacle and converted the ocean itself into a great highway of international intercourse and commerce. The early growth of her shipping and shipbuilding, coupled with the genius and energy of her merchants, the skill and daring of her seamen, the enterprise of her colonists, and the zeal of her missionaries, secured to India the command of the sea for ages, and helped her to attain and long maintain her proud position as the mistress of the Eastern seas. There was no lack of energy on the part of Indians of old in utilizing to the full the opportunities presented by nature for the development of Indian maritime activity—the fine geographical position of India in the heart of the Orient, with Africa on the west and the Eastern Archipelago and Australia on the east, her connection with the vast mainland of Asia on the north, her possession of a sea-board that extends over more than four thousand miles, and finally the network of rivers which opens up the interior. In fact, in India there is to be found the conjunction or assemblage of most of those specific geographical conditions on which depends the commercial development of a country.

II.—Evidences.

The sources and materials available for the construction of a history of Indian shipping and maritime activity naturally divide themselves into two classes, Indian and foreign. The Indian evidences are those derived from Indian literature and art, including sculpture and painting, besides the evidence of archaeology in its threefold branches, epigraphic, monumental, and numismatic. The evidences of Indian literature are based chiefly on Sanskrit, Pali, and Persian works, and in some cases on works in the Indian vernaculars, Tamil, Marathi, and Bengali. The foreign evidences consist of those writings of foreign travellers and historians which contain observations on Indian subjects, and also of archaeological remains such as those in Java. The former are embedded mostly in classical literature, in Chinese, Arabic, and Persian, to which we have access only through translations.

The way these various evidences, literary and monumental, Indian and foreign, will be arranged, and the order in which they will be presented, require to be explained at the outset. Bearing in mind the well-known dictum that "the literature as well as the art of a people tells its life," I have thought that the case for India's maritime activity cannot be held to be sufficiently made out until in the first instance it is supported by the evidence supplied by her own native literature and art, great as they are. The first proofs of Indian maritime activity, and of the existence and growth of an Indian shipping by which that activity realized itself, must accordingly be sought in the domain of Indian literature and art, and the want or paucity of these can hardly be compensated for by the abundance of evidences culled from foreign works. The evidences that will therefore be first presented will be all Indian, being those supplied by Indian literature and art, and after them will follow the evidences derived from foreign sources. Again, as the dates of most of the Indian literary works to which reference will be made are unhappily not yet a matter of certainty, I could not make the evidences drawn from them the basis of any historical treatment of the subject or regard them as any help to a chronological arrangement of the facts regarding the shipping, sea-borne trade, and maritime activity of India. Accordingly, the evidence from Indian literature that will be first adduced will serve only as an introduction to the whole subject, preparing the ground and making out the case for it, so to speak. The real historical narrative of the naval activity of India will be built up of materials supplied by such foreign and also Indian works as labour under no chronological difficulties.

The passages from ancient Indian works will be presented, as far as possible, in the order determined by tradition. In the opinion of the late Professor Bühler, the far-famed German orientalist, "there are passages in ancient Indian works which prove the early existence of a navigation of the Indian Ocean and the somewhat later occurrence of trading voyages undertaken by Hindu merchants to the shores of the Persian Gulf and its rivers." These proofs, however, will be found mostly to supply an indirect kind of evidence; they contain no direct information regarding the existence and development of a national shipping which is certainly implied in the existence, development, and continuance of that maritime trade to which they so conclusively refer. For it is a commonplace of history, and quite stands to reason, that no commerce can spring up, and much less thrive, especially in early times, unless it is fostered by a national shipping. Accordingly, the direct proofs that are available regarding Indian shipping and naval activity will have precedence over the indirect ones, and they will include illustrations of the typical ships and boats that are represented in old Indian art, in sculpture and painting, and on coins.

III.—Epochs.

The epochs of Indian history round which these various evidences regarding the shipping and maritime activity of India will be grouped, may be roughly indicated as follows:—

1. The *Pre-Mauryan Epoch*, extending from the earliest times to about the year B.C. 321.—For this period we shall discuss the evidences that can be gleaned from some of the oldest literary records of humanity like the *Ṛig-Veda*, the Bible, and some of the old Pali and Tamil works, as also from the finds of Egyptian and Assyrian archaeologists, regarding the early maritime intercourse of India with the West. Evidences for this period are also to be derived from the writings of the Greek authors Herodotus and Ctesias, in the 5th century B.C., containing references to India.

2. The *Mauryan Epoch* (B.C. 321–184).—For this period the available evidences are those preserved in the works of many Greek and Roman authors who essayed to tell the story of Alexander's Indian campaign and recorded the observations made on India by the Greek ambassadors to the courts of the Maurya emperors. These Greek and Roman notices of India have been mostly made accessible to Indian students by the translations of Mr. McCrindle. More important and interesting than these foreign evidences is the evidence fur-

nished by a recently published Sanskrit work, the *Arthaśāstra* of Kautilya, which is a mine of information regarding the manifold aspects of a highly developed material civilization witnessed by Maurya India. Bearing on this period also is the evidence of tradition preserved in that monumental work of the Kashmirian poet Kshemendra called *Bodhisattvāvadāna Kalpalatā*, which is now being published by the Asiatic Society of Bengal in the Bibliotheca Indica series. The seventy-third *pallava* or chapter of this work relates a story which throws some light on the sea-borne trade and maritime activity of India during the days of the Emperor Asoka.

3. *The Kushan Period in the north and the Andhra Period in the south*, extending roughly from the 2nd century B.C. to the 3rd century A.D.—This was the period when Roman influence on India was at its height; in fact, the whole of the southern peninsula under the Andhra dynasty was in direct communication with Rome, while the conquests in Northern India tended still further to open up trade with the Roman Empire, so that Roman gold poured into all parts of India in payment for her silks, spices, gems, and dye-stuffs. The evidences proving this are the remarkable finds of Roman coins, more numerous in the south than in the north, together with the references in the ancient Sanskrit and Pali works to "Romaka," or the city of Rome, and in ancient Tamil works to the

"Yavanas" or Greeks and Romans, and to the important South Indian ports like Muchiris and Pukar, of which full descriptions are given in old Tamil poems. Besides evidences from ancient Indian literature bearing on Indian commerce with Rome, there are also definite evidences from important foreign works. The chief of these are Pliny's *Natural History*, the *Periplus of the Erythraean Sea*, and Ptolemy's *Geography*, besides the incidental allusions to Indian commerce and shipping thrown out by writers like Agatharcides and Strabo.

4. *The Period of Hindu Imperialism in Northern India under the Guptas and Harshavardhana*, extending from the 4th century to the 7th century A.D.—This was the period of the expansion of India and of much colonizing activity towards the farther East from Bengal, the Kalinga coast, and Coromandel. Parts of Burma and Malacca were colonized, chiefly from Kalinga and Bengal, as shown in Sir A. P. Phayre's *History of Burma*, and testified to by Burmese sacred scriptures and coins. The main evidences for the remarkable maritime activity of this period are supplied by the accounts of the numerous Chinese pilgrims to India, of whom Fa-Hien was the first and Hiuen Tsang the most famous. These accounts are now all accessible through translations. Among foreign works supplying valuable materials for the history of the period may be mentioned the *Christian Topography*

of Cosmas. Some very valuable evidences regarding the early commerce between India and China are furnished by Chinese annals like the *Kwai-Yuen Catalogue* of the Chinese Tripitaka. Yule's *Cathay and the Way Thither* also has recorded many facts relating to the Indian intercourse with China. For the reign of Harsha the most important source of information is the *Travels* of Hiuen Tsang, that "treasure-house of accurate information, indispensable to every student of Indian antiquity, which has done more than any archaeological discovery to render possible the remarkable resuscitation of lost Indian history which has recently been effected."

5. *The Period of Hindu Imperialism in Southern India and the rise of the Cholas*, extending from the middle of the 7th century up to the Mahomedan conquests in Northern India.—During this period Indian maritime intercourse was equally active with both the West and the East. The colonization of Java was completed, and the great temple of Borobudur remained a standing monument of the hold which Buddhism had on that island. The field of Indian maritime enterprise was extended as far as Japan, which is testified to by Japanese tradition and official annals made accessible through the efforts of Japanese scholars like Dr. Taka-kusu. The record of I-Tsing, the famous Chinese traveller, contains many interesting details

regarding Indian maritime activity in the Eastern waters and intercourse with China in the latter half of the 7th century. Chinese annals also furnish evidences regarding the maritime intercourse of the Cholas with China, e.g. the *Sung-shih*.

6. *The Musalman (pre-Mogul) Period*, extending from the 11th century to the 15th.—The sources of evidence for this, and indeed the whole of the Musalman period, are mostly imbedded in Persian works which have been made accessible to scholars by the monumental *History of India* by Sir H. Elliot, in eight volumes. For information regarding maritime enterprise and activity in Sindh our authorities are *Al-Bilāduri* and *Chach-nāma*, translated in Elliot, vol. i. The early Musalman travellers throw much light upon Indian affairs of this period. Al-Biruni is our authority for the 11th century and Al-Idrisi for the 12th. In the 13th century a very valuable source of information regarding Indian shipping and commerce is furnished by a foreign traveller, the Venetian Marco Polo. Wassaf is our guide in the next century, as well as *Tārikh-i-Firozshāhi*. In the 15th century we have, in the Chinese account of Mahuan, the most important foreign notice of India after Marco Polo, which relates the exchange of presents between the kings of Bengal and the emperors of China. To the same century also belong the foreign travellers Abd-er-Razzak, Nicolo Conti, and Hiero-

nimo di Santo Stefano, who are also valuable sources of information regarding the shipping and trade of the period. In the earlier part of the 16th century, when the Portuguese first appear as a factor in Indian politics, details regarding Indian maritime activity are derivable from Portuguese annals like *De Coutto*, utilized in some of the standard works on the history of the Portuguese power in India. About the same time the foreign traveller Varthema has left a very interesting account of shipbuilding in Calicut.

7. *The Period of Mogul Monarchy*, from the 16th century to the 18th, i.e. from the reign of Akbar to that of Aurangzeb.—The evidence for the reign of Akbar is derived, firstly, from that mine of information, Abul-Fazl's *Ayeen-i-Akbari*, which gives a very valuable account of Akbar's Admiralty; and, secondly, from the abstract of *Ausil Toomar Jumma* given in Grant's *Analysis of the Finances of Bengal* in the *Fifth Report*, in which are contained many interesting details regarding the organization and progress of the Imperial Nowwara or shipping stationed at Dacca, the sources of revenue for its maintenance, the materials for shipbuilding, and the like. *The Chach-nāma* in Elliot, vol. i., and Abul-Fazl's *Ayeen-i-Akbari* give some details about the shipping and ports of Sindh. Some details regarding Hindu maritime activity, commerce, and shipping in Bengal are also derived

from *Takmilla-i-Akbarnāma* in Elliot, vol. vi., from the Sanskrit work *Ghataka-kārikā*, from the Portuguese accounts of De Barros and Souza, from the records of other foreign travellers like Varthema and Ralph Fitch, and lastly from some old Bengali poems and songs preserving local tradition. In the reign of Aurangzeb the principal sources of our information regarding the maritime activities of the Ferenghies and of the imperial fleet are the *Fathiyyah-i-ibriyyah*, translated by Blochmann, and the contemporary Persian *Account of Shihab-ud-dīn Talish* in MS. Bodleian 589, Sachau and Ethé's Catalogue, which is translated by Professor Jadunath Sarkar, M.A. Among foreign travellers who supply us with information for this period we may mention Thomas Bowrey, in whose account of the countries round the Bay of Bengal we have many interesting details regarding shipping and commerce. Dr. Fryer is also another similar source of our information. The same period also witnessed the development of Maratha shipping and maritime activity under Sivaji and the Peshwas, details regarding which may be derived from some of the standard works on Maratha history.

BOOK I. HINDU PERIOD.

PART I.

Indications of Maritime Activity in Indian Literature and Art.

BOOK I.—PART I.

CHAPTER I.

Direct Evidences from Sanskrit and Pali Literature.

It has been already pointed out that though Sanskrit and Pali literature abounds in references to the trading voyages of Indians, they unfortunately furnish but few references having a direct bearing on the ships and shipbuilding of India which enabled her to keep up her international connections. I have, however, been able to find one Sanskrit work,[1] which is something like a treatise on the art of shipbuilding in ancient India, setting forth many interesting details about the various sizes and kinds of ships, the materials out of which they were built, and the like; and it sums up in a condensed form all the available information and knowledge about that truly ancient industry of India. The book requires a full notice, and its contents have to be explained.

[1] It is not a printed book but a MS., to be found in the Calcutta Sanskrit College Library, called the *Yuktikalpataru*. Professor Aufrecht has noticed it in his Catalogue of Sanskrit MSS. Dr. Rajendralal Mitra has the following comment on it (*Notices of Sanskrit MSS.*, vol. i., no. CCLXXI.): "*Yuktikalpataru* is a compilation by Bhoja Narapati. It treats of jewels, swords, horses, elephants, ornaments, flags, umbrellas, seats, ministers, ships, etc., and frequently quotes from an author of the name of Bhoja, meaning probably Bhoja Rājā of Dhara."

The ancient shipbuilders had a good knowledge of the materials as well as the varieties and properties of wood which went to the making of ships. According to the *Vṛiksha-Āyurveda*, or the Science of Plant Life (Botany), four different kinds of wood [1] are to be distinguished: the first or the Brahman class comprises wood that is light and soft and can be easily joined to any other kind of wood; the second or the Kshatriya class of wood is light and hard but cannot be joined on to other classes; the wood that is soft and heavy belongs to the third or Vaisya class; while the fourth or the Sudra class of wood is characterized by both hardness and heaviness. There may also be distinguished wood of the mixed (Dvijāti) class, in which are blended properties of two separate classes.

According to Bhoja, an earlier authority on shipbuilding, a ship built of the Kshatriya class of wood brings wealth and happiness.[2] It is these ships that are to be used as means of communication where the communication is difficult owing to vast water.[3]

---

[1] लघु यत् कोमलं काष्ठं सुघटं ब्रह्मजाति तत्।
दृढाङ्गं लघु यत् काष्ठमघटं क्षत्रजाति तत्॥
कोमलं गुरु यत् काष्ठं वैश्यजाति तदुच्यते।
दृढाङ्गं गुरु यत् काष्ठं शूद्रजाति तदुच्यते॥
लक्षणद्वय योगेन द्विजातिः काष्ठ संग्रहः॥

[2] क्षत्रियकाष्ठैर्घटिता भोजमते सुखसम्पदं नौका।

[3] अन्ये लघुभिः सुदृढैर्विदधति जलदुष्पदे नौकाम्।

Ships, on the other hand, which are made of timbers of different classes possessing contrary properties are of no good and not at all comfortable. They do not last for a long time, they soon rot in water, and they are liable to split at the slightest shock and to sink down.[1]

Besides pointing out the class of wood which is best for ships, Bhoja also lays down a very important direction for shipbuilders in the nature of a warning which is worth carefully noting.[2] He says that care should be taken that no iron is used in holding or joining together the planks of bottoms intended to be sea-going vessels, for the iron will inevitably expose them to the influence of magnetic rocks in the sea, or bring them within a magnetic field and so lead them to risks. Hence the planks of bottoms are to be fitted together or mortised by means of substances other than iron. This rather quaint direction was perhaps necessary in an age when Indian ships plied in deep waters on the main.

Besides Bhoja's classification of the kinds of wood used in making ships and boats, the *Yuktikalpataru* gives an elaborate classification of the ships themselves, based on their size. The primary

---

[1] विभिन्नजातिद्वयकाष्ठजाता न श्रेयसे नापि सुखाय नौका।
नैषा चिरं तिष्ठति पच्यते च विभिद्यते सरिति मज्जते च॥

[2] न सिन्धुगाद्यार्हति लौहबन्धं तल्लोहकान्तैर्ह्रियते हि लौहम्।
विपद्यते तेन जलेषु नौका गुणेन बन्धं निजगाद भोजः॥

division[1] is into two classes: (a) *Ordinary* (Sāmānya): ships that are used in ordinary river traffic or waterways fall under this class; (b) *Special* (Viśesa), comprising only sea-going vessels. There are again enumerated ten different kinds of vessels under the Ordinary class which all differ in their lengths, breadths, and depths or heights. Below are given their names and the measurements of the three dimensions[2]:—

(*a*) Ordinary.

Names.	Length in cubits.	Breadth in cubits.	Height in cubits.
(1) Kshudrā	16	4	4
(2) Madhyamā	24	12	8
(3) Bhīmā	40	20	20
(4) Chapalā	48	24	24
(5) Patalā	64	32	32
(6) Bhayā	72	36	36
(7) Dirghā	88	44	44
(8) Patraputā	96	48	48
(9) Garbharā	112	56	56
(10) Mantharā	120	60	60

[1] सामान्यञ्च विशेषञ्च नौकाया लक्षणद्वयम् ।

[2] राजहस्तमितायामा तत्पादपरिणाहिनी ।
तावदेवोन्नता नौका क्षुद्रेति गदिता बुधैः ॥
अतः सार्द्धमितायामा तदर्द्धपरिणाहिनी ।
त्रिभागेणोत्थिता नौका मध्यमेति प्रचक्षते ॥
क्षुद्राथ मध्यमा भीमा चपला पटला भया ।
दीर्घा पत्रपुटा चैव गर्भरा मन्थरा तथा ॥
नौकादशकमित्युक्तं राजहस्तैरनुक्रमम् ।
एकैकवृद्धैः सार्द्धैश्च विजानीयाद् द्वयं द्वयम् ।
उन्नतिश्च प्रवीणा च हस्तादर्द्धांशलक्षिता ॥
अत्र भीमा भया चैव गर्भरा चाशुभप्रदा ।

Of the above ten different kinds of *Ordinary* ships the Bhīmā, Bhayā and Garbharā are liable to bring ill-luck, perhaps because their dimensions do not make them steady and well-balanced on the water.

Ships that fall under the class *Special* are all sea-going.[1] They are in the first instance divided into two sub-classes[2]: (1) Dīrghā (दीर्घा), including ships which are probably noted for their length, and (2) Unnatā (उन्नता), comprising ships noted more for their height than their length or breadth. There are again distinguished ten varieties of ships of the Dīrghā (दीर्घा) class and five of the Unnatā (उन्नता) class. Below are given their names and the measurements[3] of their respective lengths, breadths, and heights :—

(*b*) Special.

I. Dīrghā, 42 (length), 5¼ (breadth), 4⅕ (height):

Names.	Length.	Breadth.	Height.
(1) Dīrghikā	32	4	3⅕
(2) Taraṇi	48	6	4⅘
(3) Lolā	64	8	6⅖
(4) Gatvarā	80	10	8
(5) Gāmini	96	12	9⅗
(6) Tari	112	14	11⅕

[1] मन्थरापरतोयासु नासामेवाम्बुधौ गतिः ।

[2] दीर्घा चैवोन्नता चेति विशेषे द्विविधा भिदा ।

[3] राजहस्तद्वयायामा अष्टांशपरिणाहिनी ।
नौकेयं दीर्घिका नाम दशाङ्गैरुन्नतापि च ॥
दीर्घिका तरणिर्लोला गत्वरा गामिनी तरिः ।
जङ्घाला प्लाविनी चैव धारिणी वेगिनी तथा ॥
राजहस्तैकैकवृद्धा—नौकानामानि वै दश ।
उन्नतिः परिणाहश्च दशाष्टांशमितौ क्रमात् ॥

	Names.	Length.	Breadth.	Height.
(7)	Jaṅghālā	128	16	$12\frac{4}{5}$
(8)	Plābinī	144	18	$14\frac{2}{5}$
(9)	Dhāriṇī	160	20	16
(10)	Beginī	176	22	$17\frac{3}{5}$

Of these ten varieties of Dīrghā (दीर्घा) ships, those that bring ill-luck[1] are Lolā (लोला), Gāminī (गामिनी), and Plābinī (प्लाविनी), and also all ships that fall between these three classes and their next respective classes.

II. Unnatā[2] (उन्नता):

	Names.	Length.	Breadth.	Height.
(1)	Ūrddhvā	32	16	16
(2)	Anūrddhvā	48	24	24
(3)	Svarṇamukhī	64	32	32
(4)	Garbhiṇī	80	40	40
(5)	Mantharā	96	48	48

Of these five varieties, Anūrddhvā (अनूर्द्धा), Garbhiṇī (गर्भिणी), and Mantharā (मन्थरा) bring on misfortune, and Ūrddhvā much gain or profit to kings.

---

[1] अत्र लोला गामिनी च प्लाविनी दुःखदा भवेत् ।
लोलाया मानमारभ्य यावद्भवति गत्वरा ।
लोलायाः फलमाधत्ते एवं सर्व्वासु निर्णयः ॥

[2] राजहस्तद्वयमिता मानत्प्रसरचोन्नता ।
इयमूर्द्धाभिधा नौका क्षेमाय पृथिवीभुजाम् ॥
अथानूर्द्धा स्वर्णमुखी गर्भिणी मन्थरा तथा ।
राजहस्तैकैकवृद्ध्या नाम पञ्चयं भवेत् ॥
अथानूर्द्धा गर्भिणी च निन्दितं नामयुग्मकम् ।
मन्थरायाः परा यास्तु ताः शुभाय यथोद्भवम् ॥

Opinions of Sanskrit scholars whom I have consulted differ as to the exact meaning of the passages above quoted from the MS. *Yuktikalpataru*. According to some the word राजा means चन्द्र = 1, and हस्त = 2, so that राजहस्त stands for the number 21. But according to others, with whom I agree, राजा = 16, for in the works on Astronomy or ज्योतिष्, 'महीभृत' or 'राजा' is often used to indicate that number. I have made the calculations given above on the basis of the second interpretation.

The *Yuktikalpataru* also gives elaborate directions for decorating and furnishing ships so as to make them quite comfortable to passengers. Four kinds of metal are recommended for decorative purposes, viz. gold, silver, copper, and the compound of all three. Four kinds of colours are recommended respectively for four kinds of vessels: a vessel with four masts is to be painted white, that with three masts to be painted red, that with two masts is to be a yellow ship, and the one-masted ship must be painted blue. The prows of ships admit of a great variety of fanciful shapes or forms: these comprise the heads of lion, buffalo, serpent, elephant, tiger, birds such as the duck, peahen or parrot, the frog, and man, thus arguing a great development of the art of the carpenter or the sculptor. Other elements of decoration are pearls and garlands of gold to be attached to and hung from the beautifully shaped prows.[1]

[1] धात्वादीनामतो वक्ष्ये निर्णयं तरिसंश्रयम् ।
कनकं रजतं ताम्रं त्रितयं वा यथाक्रमम् ॥
मध्यादिभिः परिन्यस्य नौका चित्रककर्माणि ।
चतुःशृङ्गा त्रिशृङ्गाभा द्विशृङ्गा चैकशृङ्गिणी ॥
सितरक्तापीतनीलवर्णान् दद्याद् यथाक्रमम् ॥
केशरी महिषो नागो द्विरदो व्याघ्र एव च ।
पक्षी भेको मनुष्यश्च एतेषां वदनाष्टकम् ॥
नावां मुखे परिन्यस्य चादित्यादिदशाभुवाम् ॥
. . . . . .
नौकासु मणिविन्यासो विज्ञेयो नवदम्भवत् ।
मुक्तास्तवकैर्युक्ता नौका स्यात् सर्वतो भद्रा ।

There are also given interesting details about the cabins of ships. Three classes[1] of ships are distinguished according to the length and position of their cabins. There are firstly the Sarbamandirā (सर्व्वमन्दिरा) vessels, which have the largest cabins extending from one end of the ship to the other.[2] These ships are used for the transport of royal treasure, horses, and women.[3] Secondly, there are the Madhyamandirā (मध्यमन्दिरा) vessels,[4] which have their cabins just in the middle part. These vessels are used in pleasure trips by kings, and they are also suited for the rainy season. Thirdly, ships may have their cabins towards their prows, in which case they will be called Agramandirā[5] (अग्रमन्दिरा). These ships are used in the dry season after the rains have ceased. They are eminently suited for long voyages and also to be *used in naval warfare*.[6] It was probably in these vessels that the first naval fight recorded in Indian literature was fought, the vessel in which Tugra the Ṛishi king sent his son

---

[1] सगृहा त्रिविधा प्रोक्ता सर्व्वमध्याग्रमन्दिरा ।

[2] सर्व्वतो मन्दिरं यत्र सा ज्ञेया सर्व्वमन्दिरा ।

[3] राज्ञां कोशाश्वनारीणां यानमत्र प्रशस्यते ।

[4] मध्यतो मन्दिरं यत्र सा ज्ञेया मध्यमन्दिरा ।
राज्ञां विलासयात्रादि वर्षासु च प्रशस्यते ।

[5] अग्रतो मन्दिरं यत्र सा ज्ञेया अग्रमन्दिरा ।

[6] चिरप्रवासयात्रायां रणे काले घनात्यये ।

Bhujyu against some of his enemies in the distant island, who, being afterwards shipwrecked with all his followers on the ocean, "where there is nothing to give support, nothing to rest upon or cling to," was rescued from a watery grave by the two Asvins in their hundred-oared galley.[1] It was in a similar ship that the righteous Paṇdava brothers escaped from the destruction planned for them, following the friendly advice of kind-hearted Vidura, who kept a ship ready and constructed for the purpose, provided with all necessary machinery and weapons of war, able to defy hurricanes.[2] Of the same description were also the five hundred ships mentioned in the *Rāmāyaṇa*,[3] in which hundreds of Kaivarta young men are asked to lie in wait and obstruct the

---

[1] तुग्रोह भुज्युमश्विनोदमेघे रयिं न कश्चिन्ममृवाँ अवाहाः ।
तमूहथुर्नौभिरात्मन्वतीभिरंतरिक्ष प्रुद्भिरपोदकाभिः ॥
तिस्रः क्षपस्त्रिरहातिव्रजद्भिर्नासत्या भुज्युमूहथुः पतंगैः ।
समुद्रस्य धन्वन्नार्द्रस्य पारे त्रिभी रथैः शतपद्भिः षळश्वैः ॥
अनारंभणे तदवीरयेथामनास्थाने अग्रभणे समुद्रे ।
यदश्विना ऊहथुर्भुज्युमस्तं शतारित्रां नावमातस्थिवांसं ॥

[2] ततः प्रवासितो विद्वान् विदुरेण नरस्तदा ।
पार्थानां दर्शयामास मनोमारुतगामिनीम् ॥
सर्व्ववातसहां नावं यन्त्रयुक्तां पताकिनीम ।
शिवे भागीरथीतीरे नरैर्विश्रम्भिभिः कृताम ॥
Mahābhārata, आदिपर्व्व ।

[3] नावां शतानां पञ्चानां कैवर्त्तानां शतं शतम् ।
सन्नद्धानां तथा यूनान्तिष्ठन्त्वित्यभ्यचोदयत् ॥
Ayodhyā Kāndam.

enemy's passage. And, further, it was in these ships that the Bengalis once made a stand against the invincible prowess of Raghu as described in Kālidāsa's *Raghuvaṅsa*, who retired after planting the pillars of his victory on the isles of the holy Ganges.[1]

The conclusions as to ancient Indian ships and shipping suggested by these evidences from Sanskrit literature directly bearing on them are also confirmed by similar evidences culled from the Pali literature. The Pali literature, like the Sanskrit, also abounds with allusions to sea voyages and seaborne trade, and it would appear that the ships employed for these purposes were of quite a large size. Though indeed the Pali texts do not usually give the actual measurements of the different dimensions of ships such as the Sanskrit texts furnish, still they make definite mention of the number of passengers which the ships carried, and thus enable us in another very conclusive way to have a precise idea of their size. Thus, according to the *Rājavalliya*, the ship in which Prince Vijaya and his followers were sent away by King Siṅhaba (Siṅhavāhu) of Bengal was so large as to accommodate full seven hundred passengers, all

[1] वङ्गानुत्खाय तरसा नेता नौसाधनाद्यतान् ।
निचखान जयस्तम्भं गङ्गा स्रोतोऽन्तरेषु च ॥

Vijaya's followers.[1] Their wives and children, making up more than seven hundred, were also cast adrift in similar ships.[2] The ship in which the lion-prince, Sinhala, sailed from some unknown part of Jambudvīpa to Ceylon contained five hundred merchants besides himself.[3] The ship in which Vijaya's Pandyan bride was brought over to Ceylon was also of a very large size, for she is said to have carried no less than 800 passengers on board.[4] The *Janaka-Jātaka* mentions a ship that was wrecked with all its crew and passengers to the favourite number of seven hundred, in addition to Buddha himself in an earlier incarnation.[5] So also the ship in which Buddha in the Supparaka-Bodhisat incarnation made his voyages from Bharukaccha (Broach) to "the Sea of the Seven Gems"[6] carried seven hundred merchants besides himself. The wrecked ship of the *Vālahassa-Jātaka* carried five hundred merchants.[7] The ship which is mentioned in the *Samudda-Vanija-Jātaka* was so large as to accommodate also a whole village

---

[1] Upham's *Sacred Books of Ceylon*, ii. 28, 168. Turnour's *Mahāwanso*, 46, 47.

[2] Turnour's *Mahāwanso*, 46.

[3] *Si-yu-ki*, ii. 241.

[4] Turnour's *Mahāwanso*, 51.

[5] Bishop Bigandet's *Life of Godama*, 415.

[6] Hardy's *Manual of Buddhism*, 13.

[7] "Now it happened that five hundred shipwrecked traders were cast ashore near the city of these sea-goblins."

of absconding carpenters numbering a thousand who failed to deliver the goods (furniture, etc.) for which they had been paid in advance.[1] The ship in which the Punna brothers, merchants of Suppa-raka, sailed to the region of the red-sanders was so big that besides accommodating three hundred merchants, there was room left for the large cargo of that timber which they carried home.[2] The two Burmese merchant-brothers Tapoosa and Palekat crossed the Bay of Bengal in a ship that conveyed full five hundred cartloads of their own goods, besides whatever other cargo there may have been in it.[3] The ship in which was rescued from a watery grave the philanthropic Brahman of the *Sāṅkha-Jātaka* was 800 cubics in length, 600 cubits in width, and 20 fathoms in depth, and had three masts. The ship in which the prince of the *Mahājanaka-Jātaka* sailed with other traders from Chāmpā (modern Bhagalpur) for Suvarṇabhūmi (probably either Burma or the Golden Chersonese, or the whole Farther-Indian coast) had on board seven caravans with their beasts. Lastly, the *Dāthā dhātu wanso*, in relating the story of the conveyance of the Tooth-relic from Dantapura to Ceylon, gives an interesting description of a ship.

1 "There stood near Benares a great town of carpenters containing a thousand families." (Cambridge translation of *Jātakas*.)

2 Hardy, *Manual of Buddhism*, 57, 260.

3 Bishop Bigandet's *Life of Godama*, 101.

The royal pair (Dantakumaro and his wife) reached the port of Tamralipta, and found there "a vessel bound for Ceylon, firmly constructed with planks sewed together with ropes, having a well-rigged, lofty mast, with a spacious sail, and commanded by a skilful navigator, on the point of departure. Thereupon the two illustrious Brahmans (in disguise), in their anxiety to reach Sińhala, expeditiously made off to the vessel (in a canoe) and explained their wishes to the commander."

CHAPTER II.

Direct Evidences from Indian Sculpture, Painting, and Coins.

The conclusions pointed to by these literary evidences seem further to be supported by other kinds of evidence mainly monumental in their character. They are derived from old Indian art—from Indian sculpture and painting—and also from Indian coins. These evidences, though meagre in comparison with the available literary evidences, native and foreign alike, have, however, a compensating directness and freshness, nay, the permanence which Art confers, creating things of beauty that remain a joy for ever. Indeed, the light that is thrown on ancient Indian shipping by old Indian art is not yet extinguished, thanks to the durable character of old Indian monuments, thanks also to the labours of the Archaeological Department for their preservation and maintenance.

There are several representations of ships and boats in old Indian art. The earliest of them are those to be found among the Sanchi sculptures belonging to an age so far back as the 2nd century B.C. One of the sculptures on the Eastern Gateway of No. 1 Stupa at Sanchi represents a canoe made up of rough planks rudely sewn together by hemp

SCULPTURES FROM THE SANCHI STUPAS.

[*To face p.* 32.

or string. "It represents a river or a sheet of fresh water with a canoe crossing it, and carrying three men in the ascetic priestly costume, two propelling and steering the boat, and the central figure, with hands resting on the gunwale, facing towards four ascetics, who are standing in reverential attitude at the water's edge below."[1] According to Sir A. Cunningham,[2] the figures in the boat represent Sakya Buddha and his two principal followers; and Buddha himself has been compared in many Buddhist writings to "a boat and oar in the vast ocean of life and death."[3] But General F. C. Maisley is inclined to view this sculpture "as representing merely the departure on some expedition or mission of an ascetic, or priest, of rank amid the reverential farewells of his followers."[4] His main reasons for supporting this view are, firstly, that no representations of Buddha in human shape were resorted to until several centuries later than the date of these sculptures; and, secondly, because the representation is that of a common thong-bound canoe and not of a sacred barge suiting the great Buddha. There is another sculpture to be found on the Western Gateway of No. I Stupa at Sanchi which "represents a piece of water, with a barge

---

[1] General F. C. Maisley, *Sanchi and its Remains*, p. 42.

[2] *The Bhilsa Topes*, 27.

[3] *Foe-koue-ki*, ch. xxiv., note 11.

[4] *Sanchi and its Remains*, p. 43.

floating on it whose prow is formed by a winged gryphon and stern by a fish's tail. The barge contains a pavilion overshadowing a vacant throne, over which a male attendant holds a *chatta*, while another man has a *chaori;* a third man is steering or propelling the vessel with a large paddle. In the water are fresh-water flowers and buds and a large shell; and there are five men floating about, holding on by spars and inflated skins, while a sixth appears to be asking the occupant of the stern of the vessel for help out of the water."[1] This sculpture appears simply to represent the royal state barge, which quite anticipates its modern successors used by Indian nobles at the present day, and the scene is that of the king and some of his courtiers disporting themselves in an artificial piece of water; but it is also capable of a symbolical meaning, especially when we consider that the shape of the barge here shown is that of the sacred *Makara*, the fish avatara or Jataka of the Buddhist, just as the Hindu scriptures make the *Matsya*, or fish, the first of the avatars of Vishnu, whose latest incarnation was Buddha. According to Lieutenant Massey, however, this sculpture represents the conveyance of relics from India to Ceylon which is intercepted by Nagas.[2]

In passing it may be noted that the grotesque

---

[1] *Sanchi and its Remains*, p. 59.

[2] Mrs. Spier's *Life in Ancient India*, p. 320.

and fanciful shapes given to the prow herein represented are not the invention or innovation of an ingenious sculptor trying his wit in original design; they are strictly traditional, and conform to established standards,[1] and are therefore identical with one or other of those possible forms of the prow of a ship which have been preserved for us in the slokas of the Sanskrit work *Yuktikalpataru* quoted and referred to above.

Next to Sanchi sculptures in point of time we may mention the sculptures in the caves of Kanhery in the small island of Salsette near Bombay, belonging, according to the unerring testimony of their inscriptions, to the 2nd century A.D., the time of the Andhrabhritya or S'atakarni king Vashishthiputra (A.D. 133–162) and of Gotamiputra II. (A.D. 177–196). Among these sculptures there is a representation of a scene of shipwreck on the sea and two persons helplessly praying for rescue to god Padmapani who sends two messengers for the purpose. This is perhaps the oldest representation of a sea voyage in Indian sculpture.[2]

I have come across other representations of ships and boats in Indian sculpture and painting.

---

[1] The identity of the form of the prow of the Sanchi barge with that given in the *Yuktikalpataru* may incline one to hazard the conjecture that the work may be compiled from works at least as old as the Sanchi monument, or at any rate the portions treating of prows.

[2] See *Bombay Gazetteer*, vol. xiv., p. 165.

In the course of a journey I made through Orissa and South India I noticed among the sculptures of the Temple of Jagannath at Puri a fine, well-preserved representation of a royal barge shown in relief on stone, of which I got a sketch made. The representation appears on that portion of the great Temple of Jagannath which is said to have been once a part of the Black Pagoda of Kanaraka belonging to the 12th century A.D. The sculpture shows in splendid relief a stately barge propelled by lusty oarsmen with all their might, and one almost hears the very splash of their oars; the water through which it cuts its way is thrown into ripples and waves indicated by a few simple and yet masterly touches; and the entire scene is one of dash and hurry indicative of the desperate speed of a flight or escape from danger. The beauty of the cabin and the simplicity of its design are particularly noticeable; the rocking-seat within is quite an innovation, probably meant to be effective against sea-sickness, while an equally ingenious idea is that of the rope or chain which hangs from the top and is grasped by the hand by the master of the vessel to steady himself on the rolling waters. It is difficult to ascertain what particular scene from our Shastras is here represented. It is very probably not a mere secular picture meant as an ornament. The interpretation put upon it by one of the many priests of whom I inquired, and which seems most

THE ROYAL BARGE ON THE JAGANNATH TEMPLE, PURI.

VAITAL DEUL.

[To face p. 36.

likely, being suggested by the surrounding sculptures, was that the scene represented S'rī Krishña being secretly and hurriedly carried away beyond the destructive reach of King Kańsa. It will also be remembered that the vessel herein represented is that of the Madhyamandirā type as defined in the *Yuktikalpataru*.

In Bhubaneshwara there is an old temple on the west side of the tank of Vindusârovara which requires to be noticed in this connection. The temple is called *Vaitāl Deul* after the peculiar form of its roof resembling a ship or boat capsized, the word *vaitāra* denoting a ship. The roof is more in the style of some of the Dravidian temples of Southern India, notably the *raths* of Mahavellipore, than of Orissan architecture.

There are a few very fine representations of old Indian ships and boats among the far-famed paintings of the Buddhist cave-temples at Ajantā, whither the devotees of Buddhism, nineteen centuries or more ago, retreated from the distracting cares of the world to give themselves up to contemplation. There for centuries the wild ravine and the basaltic rocks were the scene of an application of labour, skill, perseverance, and endurance that went to the excavation of these painted palaces, standing to this day as monuments of a boldness of conception and a defiance of difficulty as possible, we believe, to the modern as to the ancient Indian character. The worth of the achievement will be further evident from the fact that "much of the work has been carried on with the help of artificial light, and no great stretch of imagination is necessary to picture all that this involves in the Indian climate and in situations where thorough ventilation is impossible."[1] About the truth and precision of the work, which are no less admirable than its boldness and extent, Mr. Griffiths has the following glowing testimony:—

> During my long and careful study of the caves I have not been able to detect a single instance where a mistake has been made by cutting away too much stone; for if once a slip of this kind occurred, it could only have been repaired by the insertion of a piece which would have been a blemish.[2]

According to the best information, the execution of these works is supposed to have extended from the 2nd century B.C. to the 7th or the 8th century A.D., covering a period of more than a thousand years. The earliest caves, namely the numbers 13, 12, 10, 9, 8, arranged in the order of their age, were made under the Andhrabhrityas or S'ātakarni kings in the 2nd and 1st centuries B.C., and the date of the latest ones, namely the numbers 1–5, is placed between 525–650 A.D. By the time of Hiuen Tsang's visit their execution was completed. Hiuen Tsang's is the earliest recorded reference

[1] J. Griffiths, *The Paintings in the Buddhist Cave-Temples of Ajanta.*
[2] *Ibid.*

we have to these caves. The Chinese pilgrim did not himself visit Ajantā, but he was at the capital of Pulakeshi II., King of Mahārāstra, where he heard that "on the eastern frontier of the country is a great mountain with towering crags and a continuous stretch of piled-up rocks and scarped precipice. In this there is a Sangharam (monastery) constructed in a dark valley. . . . On the four sides of the Vihara, on the stone walls, are painted different scenes in the life of the Tathagata's preparatory life as a Bodhisattva. . . . These scenes have been cut out with the greatest accuracy and finish."[1]

The representations of ships and boats furnished by Ajantā paintings are mostly in Cave No. 2, of which the date is, as we have seen, placed between 525–650 A.D. These were the closing years of the age which witnessed the expansion of India and the spread of Indian thought and culture over the greater part of the Asiatic continent. The vitality and individuality of Indian civilization were already fully developed during the spacious times of Gupta imperialism, which about the end of the 7th century even transplanted itself to the farther East, aiding in the civilization of Java, Cambodia, Siam, China, and even Japan. After the passing away of the Gupta Empire, the government of India was in the

[1] Beal, *Buddhist Records of the Western World*, vol. ii., p. 257.

opening of the 7th century A.D. divided between Harshavardhana of Kanauj and Pulakeshi II. of the Deccan, both of whom carried on extensive intercourse with foreign countries. The fame of Pulakeshi spread beyond the limits of India and "reached the ears of Khusru II., King of Persia, who in the thirty-sixth year of his reign, 625–6 A.D., even received a complimentary embassy from Pulakeshi. The courtesy was reciprocated by a return embassy sent from Persia, which was received in the Indian court with due honour."[1] There is a large fresco painting in the Cave No. 1 at Ajantā which is still easily recognizable as a vivid representation of the ceremonial attending the presentation of their credentials by the Persian envoys.

As might be naturally expected, it was also the golden age of India's maritime activity which is reflected, though dimly, in the national art of the period. The imperial fleet was thoroughly organized, consisting of hundreds of ships; and a naval invasion of Pulakeshi II. reduced Puri, "which was the mistress of the Western seas."[2] About this time, as has been already hinted at, swarms of daring adventurers from Gujarat ports, anticipating the enterprise of the Drakes and Frobishers, or more properly of the Pilgrim Fathers,

[1] Vincent A. Smith, *Early History of India*, pp. 384, 385.

[2] See Dr. Bhandarkar's *Early History of the Deccan*, ch. x.

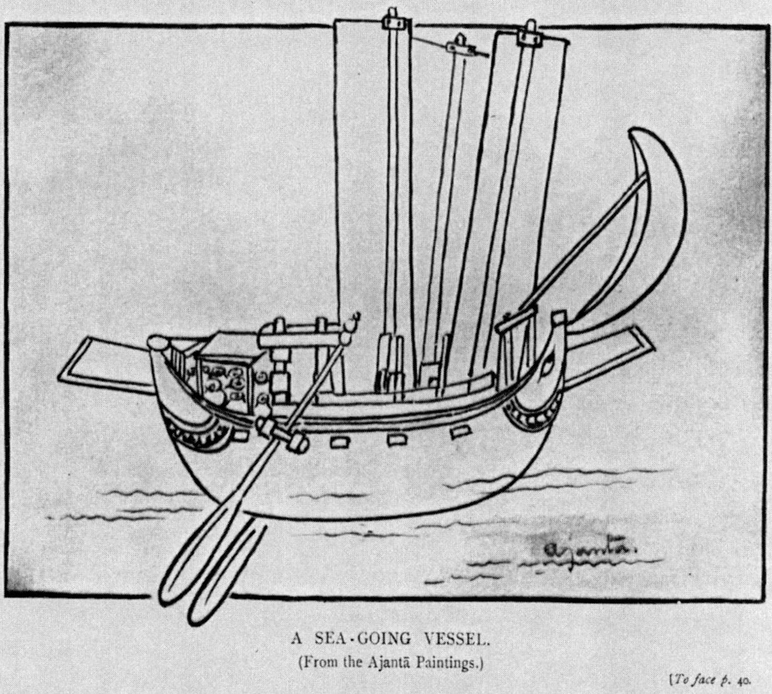

A SEA-GOING VESSEL.
(From the Ajantā Paintings.)

[To face p. 40.

sailed in search of plenty till the shores of Java arrested their progress and gave scope to their colonizing ambition.

The representations of ships and boats in the Ajantā paintings are therefore rightly interpreted by Griffiths as only a "vivid testimony to the ancient foreign trade of India." Of the two representations herein reproduced, the first shows "a sea-going vessel with high stem and stern, with three oblong sails attached to as many upright masts. Each mast is surmounted by a truck, and there is carried a lug-sail. The jib is well filled with wind. A sort of bowsprit, projecting from a kind of gallows on deck, is indicated with the out-flying jib, square in form," like that borne till recent times by European vessels. The ship appears to be decked and has ports. Steering-oars hang in sockets or rowlocks on the quarter, and eyes are painted on the bows. There is also an oar behind; and under the awning are a number of jars, while two small platforms project fore and aft.[1] The vessel is of the Agramandirā type as defined in the *Yuktikalpataru*, our Sanskrit treatise on ships.

The second representation is that of the emperor's pleasure-boat, which is "like the heraldic lymphad, with painted eyes at stem and stern, a pillared canopy amidships, and an umbrella forward,

[1] Griffiths, *The Paintings in the Buddhist Cave-Temples of Ajanta*, p. 17.

the steersman being accommodated on a sort of ladder which remotely suggests the steersman's chair in the modern Burmese row-boats; while a rower is in the bows."[1] The vessel is of the Madhyamandirā type, and corresponds exactly to the form of those vessels which, according to the *Yukti-kalpataru*, are to be used in pleasure trips by kings.

The third representation from the Ajantā paintings reproduced here is that of the scene of the landing of Vijaya in Ceylon, with his army and fleet, and his installation. The circumstances of Vijaya's banishment from Bengal with all his followers and their families are fully set forth in the Pali works, *Mahāwaṅso*, *Rājāvalliya*, and the like. The fleet of Vijaya carried no less than 1,500 passengers. After touching at several places which, according to some authorities, lay on the western coast of the Deccan, the fleet reached the shores of Ceylon, approaching the island from the southern side. The date of Vijaya's landing in Ceylon is said to have been the very day on which another very important event happened in the far-off fatherland of Vijaya, for it was the day on which the Buddha attained the Nirvāṇa. Vijaya was next installed as king, and he became the founder of the "Great Dynasty."

---

[1] Griffiths, *The Paintings in the Buddhist Cave-Temples of Ajanta*, p. 17.

THE ROYAL PLEASURE-BOAT.
(From the Ajantā Paintings.)

[*To face p. 42.*

The conquest of Ceylon, laying as it did the foundation of a Greater India, was a national achievement that was calculated to stir deeply the popular mind, and was naturally seized by the imagination of the artist as a fit theme for the exercise of his powers. It is thus that we can explain its place in our national gallery at Ajantā as we can explain that of another similar representation suggestive of India's position in the Asiatic political system of old—I mean the representation of Pulakeshi II. receiving the Persian embassy. Truly, Ajantā unfolds some of the forgotten chapters of Indian history.

The explanation of the complex picture before us can best be given after Mr. Griffiths, than whom no one is more competent to speak on the subject. On the left of the picture, issuing from a gateway, is a chief on his great white elephant, with a bow in his hand; and two minor chiefs, likewise on elephants, each shadowed by an umbrella. They are accompanied by a retinue of foot-soldiers, some of whom bear banners and spears and others swords and shields. The drivers of the elephants, with goads in their hands, are seated, in the usual manner, on the necks of the animals. Sheaves of arrows are attached to the sides of the howdahs. The men are dressed in tightly-fitting short-sleeved jackets, and loin-cloths with long ends hanging behind in folds. Below, four soldiers on horseback with spears are in a boat, and to the right are represented again the group on their elephants, also in boats, engaged in battle, as the principal figures have just discharged their bows. The elephants sway their trunks about, as is their wont when excited. The near one is shown in the act of trumpeting, and the swing of his bell indicates motion. "These may be thought open to the criticism on Raphael's cartoon of the Draught of Fishes, viz. that his boat is too small to carry his figures. The Indian artist has used Raphael's treatment for Raphael's reason; preferring, by reduced and conventional indication of the inanimate and merely accessory vessels, to find space for expression, intelligible to his public, of the elephants and horses and their riders necessary to his story."

Vijaya Sińha, according to legend, went (B.C. 543) to Ceylon with a large following. The Rakshasis or female demons inhabiting it captivated them by their charms; but Vijaya, warned in a dream, escaped on a wonderful horse. He collected an army, gave each soldier a magic verse (*mantra*), and returned. Falling upon the demons with great impetuosity, he totally routed them, some fleeing the island and others being drowned in the sea. He destroyed their town, and established himself as king in the island, to which he gave the name of Sińhala.[1]

---

[1] See Turnour's *Mahāwańso*, chs. 6–8.

LANDING OF VIJAYA IN CEYLON (ABOUT 543 B.C.).

[*To face p.* 44.

I shall now present a very important and interesting series of representations of ships which are found not in India but far away from her, among the magnificent sculptures of the Temple of Borobudur in Java, where Indian art reached its highest expression amid the Indian environment and civilization transplanted there.

Most of the sculptures show in splendid relief ships in full sail and scenes recalling the history of the colonization of Java by Indians in the earlier centuries of the Christian era. Of one of them Mr. Havell[1] thus speaks in appreciation: "The ship, magnificent in design and movement, is a masterpiece in itself. It tells more plainly than words the perils which the Prince of Gujarat and his companions encountered on the long and difficult voyages from the west coast of India. But these are over now. The sailors are hastening to furl the sails and bring the ship to anchor." There are other ships which appear to be sailing tempest-tossed on the ocean, fully trying the pluck and dexterity of the oarsmen, sailors, and pilots, who, however, in their movements and looks impress us with the idea that they are quite equal to the occasion. These sculptured types of a 6th or 7th century Indian ship—and it is the characteristic of Indian art to represent conventional forms or

---

[1] E. B. Havell's *Indian Sculpture and Painting*, p. 124.

types rather than individual things—carry our mind back to the beginning of the 5th century A.D., when a similar vessel also touched the shores of Java after a more than three months' continuous sail from Ceylon with 200 passengers on board including the famous Chinese pilgrim Fa-Hien. It is noteworthy that "astern of the great ship was a smaller one as a provision in case of the larger vessel being injured or wrecked during the voyage."[1]

The form of these ships closely resembles that of a catamaran, and somewhat answers to the following description of some Indian ships given by Nicolo Conti in the earlier part of the 15th century: "The natives of India build some ships larger than ours, capable of containing 2,000 butts, and with five sails and as many masts. The lower part is constructed with triple planks, in order to withstand the force of the tempests to which they are much exposed. But some ships are so built in compartments that should one part be shattered the other portion remaining entire may accomplish the voyage."[2]

These ships will be found to present two types of vessels. To the first type belong Nos. 1, 3, 5, 6. They are generally longer and broader than the

[1] Beal, *Buddhist Records*, vol. ii., p. 269.

[2] *India in the Fifteenth Century*, in the Hakluyt Society publications, ii., p. 27.

INDIAN ADVENTURERS SAILING OUT TO COLONIZE JAVA.
No. 1. (Reproduced from the Sculptures of Borobudur.)

INDIAN ADVENTURERS SAILING OUT TO COLONIZE JAVA.
No. 2. (Reproduced from the Sculptures of Borobudur.)

[To face p. 46.

vessels of the second type, have more than one mast, are many-ribbed, the ribs being curved, not straight. These vessels are built so narrow and top-heavy that it is necessary to fit outriggers for safety. An outrigger is a series of planks or logs joined to the boat with long poles or spars as shown in Fig. 1. It is customary when a large amount of sail is being carried for the crew to go out and stand on the outrigger as shown in Fig. 5.

No. 1 has got two masts and one long sail. No. 3 has got square sails and one stay-sail in front. In No. 5 the crew appear to be setting sail or taking sail down. No. 6 has been interpreted by Mr. Havell as representing sailors "hastening to furl the sails and bring the ship to anchor," but this suggestion seems to be contradicted by the sea-gulls or albatrosses of the sculpture flying around the vessel, which without doubt indicate that the ship is in mid-ocean, far away from land.

No. 1 shows probably a wooden figure-head and not a man; so also do Nos. 3, 5, 6. There is also a sort of cabin in each of the vessels of the first type. Again, in No. 1 the figure aft appears to be a compass.[1]

---

[1] This is the suggestion of a European expert, Mr. J. L. Reid, member of the Institute of Naval Architects and Shipbuilders, England, at present Superintendent of the Hugli Docks, Salkea (Howrah). In connection with Mr. Reid's suggestion, the following extract from the *Bombay Gazetteer*, vol. xiii., Part ii., Appendix A, will be interesting: "The early Hindu

No. 5 appears to be in collision with some other vessel, or perhaps it shows a smaller vessel which used to be carried as a provision against damages or injury to the larger one from the perils of navigation. This was, as already pointed out, true of the merchantman in which Fa-Hien took passage from Ceylon to Java. No. 5 illustrates also the use of streamers to indicate the direction of winds.

There is another type of ships represented in Nos. 2 and 4. The fronts are less curved than in the first type; there is also only one mast. No. 2 shows a scene of rescue, a drowning man being helped out of the water by his comrade. No. 4 represents a merrier scene, the party disporting themselves in catching fish.

Some of the favourite devices of Indian sculpture to indicate water may be here noticed. Fresh and sea waters are invariably and unmistakably indicated by fishes, lotuses, aquatic leaves, and the like. The *makara*, or alligator, showing its fearful row of teeth in Fig. 2, is used to indicate the ocean; so also are the albatrosses or sea-gulls of Fig. 6. The curved lines are used to indicate waves.

---

astrologers are said to have used the magnet as they still use the modern compass, in fixing the North and East, in laying foundations, and other religious ceremonies. The Hindu compass was an *iron fish* that floated in a vessel of oil and pointed to the North. The fact of this older Hindu compass seems placed beyond doubt by the Sanskrit word *maccha-yantra*, or fish machine, which Molesworth gives as a name for the mariner's compass."

INDIAN ADVENTURERS SAILING OUT TO COLONIZE JAVA.
No. 3. (Reproduced from the Sculptures of Borobudur.)

INDIAN ADVENTURERS SAILING OUT TO COLONIZE JAVA.
No. 4. (Reproduced from the Sculptures of Borobudur.)

[To face p. 48.

INDIAN ADVENTURERS SAILING OUT TO COLONIZE JAVA.
No. 5. (Reproduced from the Sculptures of Borobudur.)

INDIAN ADVENTURERS SAILING OUT TO COLONIZE JAVA.
No. 6. (Reproduced from the Sculptures of Borobudur.)

[*To face p.* 48.

The trees and pillars appear probably to demarcate one scene from another in the sculpture.

Finally, in the Philadelphia Museum there is a most interesting exhibit of the model of one of these Hindu-Javanese ships, an "outrigger ship," with the following notes :—

> Length 60 feet. Breadth 15 feet. . . .
>
> Method of construction.—A cage-work of timber above a great log answering for a keel, the hold of the vessel being formed by planking inside the timbers; and the whole being so top-heavy as to make the outrigger essential for safety.
>
> Reproduced from the frieze of the great Buddhist temple at Borobudur, Java, which dates probably from the 7th century A.D. About 600 A.D. there was a great migration from Guzarat in ancient India near the mouths of the Indus to the island of Java, due perhaps to the devastation of Upper India by Scythian tribes and to the drying up of the country.[1]

Lastly, it may be mentioned that in the Great Temple at Madura, among the fresco paintings that cover the walls of the corridors round the Suvarṇapushkariṇī tank, there is a fine representation of the sea and of a ship in full sail on the main as large as those among the sculptures of Borobudur.

We shall now refer to the available numismatic evidence bearing on Indian shipping; for besides the representations of ships and boats in Indian

---

[1] The Javanese chronicles relate that about A.D. 603 a ruler of Gujarat, forewarned of the coming destruction of his kingdom, started his son with 5,000 followers, among whom were cultivators, artisans, warriors, physicians, and writers, in 6 large and 100 small vessels, for Java, where they laid the foundation of a civilization that has given to the world the Sculptures of Borobudur.

sculpture and painting, there are a few interesting representations on some old Indian coins which point unmistakably to the development of Indian shipping and naval activity. Thus there has been a remarkable find of some Andhra coins on the east coast, belonging to the 2nd and 3rd century A.D., on which is to be detected the device of a two-masted ship, "evidently of large size." With regard to the meaning of the device Mr. Vincent Smith has thus remarked: "Some pieces bearing the figure of a ship suggest the inference that Yajña S'rī's (A.D. 184–213) power was not confined to the land."[1] Again: "The ship-coins, perhaps struck by Yajña S'rī, testify to the existence of a sea-borne trade on the Coromandel coast in the 1st century of the Christian era."[2] This inference is, of course, amply supported by what we know of the history of the Andhras, in whose times, according to R. Sewell, "there was trade both by sea and overland with Western Asia, Greece, Rome, and Egypt, as well as China and the East."[3]

In his *South Indian Buddhist Antiquities*,[4] Alexander Rea gives illustrations and descriptions of three of these ship-coins of the Andhras. They

---

[1] *Early History of India*, p. 202.

[2] *Z.D.M.G.*, p. 613. (On Andhra Coinage.)

[3] *Imperial Gazetteer*, New Edition, vol. ii., p. 825.

[4] *Archaeological Survey of India*, New Imperial Series, xv., p. 29.

No. 1.

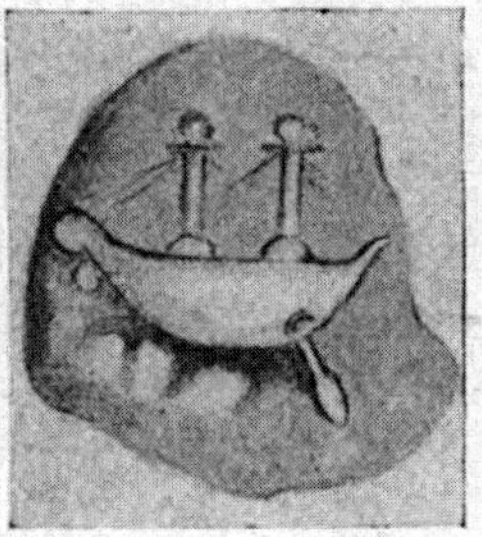

No. 2.

No. 3.

No. 4.

ANDHRA SHIP-COINS OF THE SECOND CENTURY A.D.

[*To face p.* 51.

are all of lead, weighing respectively 101 grains, 65 grains, and 29 grains. The obverse of the first shows a ship resembling the Indian *dhoni*, with bow to the right. The vessel is pointed in vertical section at each end. On the point of the stem is a round ball. The rudder, in the shape of a post with spoon on end, projects below. The deck is straight, and on it are two round objects from which rise two masts, each with a cross-tree at the top. Traces of rigging can be faintly seen. The obverse of the second shows a ship to the right. The device resembles that of the first, but the features are not quite distinct. The deck in the specimen is curved. The obverse of the third represents a device similar to the preceding, showing even more distinctly than the first. The rigging is crossed between the masts. On the right of the vessel appear three balls, and under the side are two spoon-shaped oars. No. 45 in the plate of Sir Walter Elliot's *Coins of Southern India* is also a coin of lead with a two-masted ship on the obverse.

Besides these Andhra coins there have been discovered some Kurumbar or Pallava coins on the Coromandel coast, on the reverse of which there is a figure of a "two-masted ship like the modern coasting vessel or *d'honi*, steered by means of oars from the stern." The Kurumbars were a pastoral tribe living in associated communities and inhabiting for some hundred years before the 7th century "the country from the base of the tableland to the Palar and Pennar Rivers. . . . They are stated to have been engaged in trade, and to have owned ships and carried on a considerable commerce by sea."[1]

---

[1] Sir Walter Elliot in the *Numismata Orientalia*, vol. iii., Part ii., pp. 36, 37. (Coins of Southern India.)

HINDU PERIOD

CHAPTER III.

Indirect Evidences: References and Allusions to Indian Maritime Activity in Sanskrit and Pali Literature.

I have already said that though ancient Indian literature furnishes rather meagre evidences directly bearing on Indian shipping and shipbuilding, it abounds with innumerable references to sea voyages and sea-borne trade and the constant use of the ocean as the great highway of international intercourse and commerce; which therefore serve as indirect evidence pointing to the existence and development of a national shipping, feeding and supporting a national commerce. We shall therefore now adduce those passages in ancient Indian works which, in Bühler's[1] opinion, "prove the early existence of a complete navigation of the Indian Ocean, and of the trading voyages of Indians." The oldest evidence on record is supplied by the *Ṛig-Veda*, which contains several references to sea voyages undertaken for commercial and other purposes. One passage (I. 25. 7) represents Varuṇa having a full knowledge of the ocean routes along which vessels sail. Another (II. 48. 3) speaks of merchants, under the influence of greed, sending out ships to foreign countries. A third passage (I. 56. 2)

[1] *Origin of the Indian Brahma Alphabet*, p. 84.

mentions merchants whose field of activity knows no bounds, who go everywhere in pursuit of gain, and frequent every part of the sea. The fourth passage (VII. 88. 3 and 4) alludes to a voyage undertaken by Vaśiṣtha and Varuṇa in a ship skilfully fitted out, and their "undulating happily in the prosperous swing." The fifth, which is the most interesting passage (I. 116. 3), mentions a naval expedition on which Tugra the Ṛishi king sent his son Bhujyu against some of his enemies in the distant islands; Bhujyu, however, is shipwrecked by a storm, with all his followers, on the ocean, "where there is no support, no rest for the foot or the hand," from which he is rescued by the twin brethren, the Asvins, in their *hundred-oared galley*.[1]

---

[1] The five passages are :—

वेदा यो वीनां पदमन्तरिक्षेण पततां । वेद नावः समुद्रियः ॥
(I. 25. 7.)

उवासोषा उच्छाच्च नु देवी जीरा रथानां ।
ये अस्या आचरणेषु दध्रिरे समुद्रे न श्रवस्यवः ॥
(I. 48. 3.)

तं गूर्तयो नेमन्निषः परीणसः समुद्रं न संचरणे सनिष्यवः ।
पतिं दक्षस्य विदथस्य नू सहो गिरिं न वेना अधिरोह तेजसा ॥
(I. 56. 2.)

आ यद्रुहाव वरुणश्च नावं प्र यत् समुद्रमीरयाव मध्यं ।
अधि यदपां स्नुभिश्चराव प्र प्रेंख ईंखयावहै शुभे कं ॥
वसिष्ठं ह वरुणो नाव्याधादृषिं चकार स्वपा महोभिः ।
स्तोतारं विप्रः सुदिनत्वे अह्नां यान्नु द्यावस्ततनन्यादुषासः ॥
(VII. 88. 3 & 4.)

तुग्रो ह भुज्युमश्विनोदमेघे रयिं न कश्चिन्ममृवाँ अवाहाः ।
तमूहथुर्नौभिरात्मन्वतीभिरन्तरिक्षप्रुद्भिरपोदकाभिः ॥
(I. 116. 3.)

Among other passages may be mentioned that which invokes Agni thus: "Do thou whose countenance is turned to all sides send off our adversaries as if in a ship to the opposite shore; do thou convey us in a ship across the sea for our welfare"; or that in which Agni is prayed to bestow a boat with oars.

The *Rāmāyaṇa* also contains several passages which indicate the intercourse between India and distant lands by way of the sea. In the *Kishkindhyā Kāndam*, Sugrīva, the Lord of the Monkeys, in giving directions to monkey leaders for the quest of Sītā, mentions all possible places where Rāvaṇa could have concealed her. In one passage he asks them to go to the cities and mountains in the islands of the sea[1]; in another the land of the Kosakaras[2]

---

[1] The passage in question is: समुद्रमवगाढांश्च पर्व्वतान् पत्तनानि च । (*Kishkindhyā Kāndam*, 40. 25.)

[2] The passage in question is: भूमिञ्च कोषकाराणां भूमिञ्च रजताकराम्। (*Kishkindhyā Kāndam*, 40. 23.) The commentator explains कोषकाराणां भूमिम् as कौषेयतन्तूत्पादकजन्तूत्पत्तिस्थानभूतानां भूमिम् or the land where grows the worm which yields the threads of silken clothes. The silken cloth for which China has been famous from time immemorial has been termed in Sanskrit literature चीनांशुक and चीनचेल to point to the place of its origin. Thus in Kālidāsa's *Sakuntalā* we come across the following passage:—

गच्छति पुरः शरीरं धावति पश्चादसंस्थितं चेतः ।
चीनांशुकमिव केतोः प्रतिवातं नीयमानस्य ॥

In the *Yātrātattva* of Raghunandana we find the following:—

सर्व्वांश्चमनुलिप्येच्च चन्दनेन्दुमृदुद्रवैः ।
सुगन्धि माल्याभरणैश्चीनचेलैः सुशोभनैः ॥

The following further evidence of a Western scholar may be adduced to

is mentioned as the likely place of Sītā's concealment, which is generally interpreted to be no other country than China; a third passage[1] refers to the Yavana Dvīpa and Suvarṇa Dvīpa, which are usually identified with the islands of Java and Sumatra of the Malaya Archipelago; while the fourth passage alludes to the Lohita Sāgara or the

---

show that China was the prime producer of silk: "The manufacture of silk amongst the Chinese claims a high antiquity, native authorities tracing it as a national industry for a period of five thousand years. From China the looms of Persia and of Tyre were supplied with raw silk, and through these states the Greeks and the Romans obtained the envied luxury of silk tissues. The introduction of silkworm eggs into Europe was due to two missionaries who brought them concealed in a bamboo to Byzantium. The food also of the silkworm, the white mulberry (*Morus alba*), is of Chinese origin." (*Growth and Vicissitude of Commerce*, by J. Yeats, LL.D., F.G.S., F.S.S., etc.) The same author, in his *Technical History of Commerce*, p. 149, says: "Fabrics of silk and cotton are of Oriental origin. For 600 years after its introduction from China (A.D. 552), silk cultivation was isolated within the Byzantine Empire. The rearing of the worms and the weaving of the silk was practised in Sicily during the 12th and in Italy during the 13th century, whence it was subsequently introduced into France and Spain."

[1] The passages alluded to are:—

यत्नवन्तो यवद्वीपं सप्तराज्योपशोभितम् ।
सुवर्णरूप्यकद्वीपं सुवर्णाकरमण्डितम् ॥

*　　*　　*

ततो रक्तजलं भीमं लोहितं नाम सागरम् ।

Ptolemy adopted the Sanskrit name of the island of Java and mentioned its Greek equivalent, while modern writers like Humboldt call it the Barley Island. Alberuni also has remarked that the Hindus call the islands of the Malay Archipelago by the general name of Suvarna Island, which has been interpreted by the renowned French antiquarian Reinaud to mean the islands of Java and Sumatra. (*Journal Asiatique*, tome iv., IVe Série, p. 265.)

red sea. In the *Ayodhyā Kāndam* there is even a passage which hints at preparations for a naval fight,[1] thus indirectly indicating a thorough knowledge and a universal use of waterway. The *Rāmāyaṇa* also mentions merchants who trafficked beyond the sea and were in the habit of bringing presents to the king.

In the *Mahābhārata* the accounts of the Rājasūya sacrifice and the Digvijaya of Arjuna and Nakula mention various countries outside India with which she had intercourse. There is a passage in its *Sabhā Parva* which states how Sahadeva, the youngest brother of the five Pāṇdavas, went to the several islands in the sea and conquered the Mlechchha inhabitants thereof.[2] The well-known

---

[1] नावां शतानां पञ्चानां कैवर्तानां शतं शतं ।
सन्नद्धानां तथा यूनान्तिष्ठन्त्वित्यभ्यचोदयत् ॥

(*Ayodhyā Kāndam*, 84. 78.)

[Let hundreds of Kaivarta young men lie in wait in five hundred ships (to obstruct the enemy's passage).]

The following sloka from *Manusaṁhitā*, while enumerating the various and possible methods and means of warfare, includes also naval fight by means of ships :—

स्यन्दनाश्वैः समे युध्येदनूपे नौद्विपैस्तथा ।
वृक्षगुल्मावृते चापैरसिचर्मायुधैः स्थले ॥

(*Manu*, 7. 192.)

[2] सागरद्वीपवासांश्च नृपतीन् म्लेच्छयोनिजान् ।
निषादान् पुरुषादांश्च कर्णप्रावरणानपि
द्वीपं ताम्राह्वयञ्चैव स नृपं वशे कृत्वा महामतिः ।

[The magnanimous Sahadeva conquered and brought under his subjection the Mlechchha kings and hunters and cannibals inhabiting the several islands in the sea, including the island called Tāmra, etc.]

story of the churning of the ocean, in the *Mahābhārata*, in the boldness of its conception is not without a significance. In the *Droṇa Parva* there is a passage alluding to shipwrecked sailors who "are safe if they get to an island."[1] In the same *Parva* there is another passage in which there is a reference to a "tempest-tossed and damaged vessel in a wide ocean."[2] In the *Karṇa Parva* we find the soldiers of the Kauravas bewildered like the merchants "whose ships have come to grief in the midst of the unfathomable deep."[3] There is another sloka in the same *Parva* which describes how the sons of Draupadī rescued their maternal uncles by supplying them with chariots, "as the shipwrecked merchants are rescued by means of boats." In the *S'ānti Parva* the salvation attained by means of Karma and true knowledge is compared to the gain which a merchant derives from sea-borne trade.[4] But the most interesting passage in the *Mahābhārata* is that which refers to the escape of

---

[1] भिन्ननौका यथा राजन् द्वीपमासाद्य निर्वृताः ।
भवन्ति पुरुषव्याघ्र नाविकाः कालपर्यये ॥

[2] विष्वग्वाताहता रुग्णा नौरिवासीन्महार्णवे ।

[3] निमज्जतस्तानथ कर्णसागरे
विपन्ननावो वणिजो यथार्णवात् ।
उद्दध्रिरे नौभिरिवार्णवाद्रथैः
सुकल्पितैर्द्रौपदिजाः स्वमातुलान् ॥

[4] वणिक् यथा समुद्राद्वैयथार्थम् लभते धनम्
तथा मर्त्यार्णवे जन्तोः कर्म्मविज्ञानतो गतिः ॥

the Pāṇḍava brothers from the destruction planned for them in a ship that was secretly and specially constructed for the purpose under orders of the kind-hearted Vidura.[1] The ship was of a large size, provided with machinery and all kinds of weapons of war, and able to defy storms and waves.

But besides the epics, the vast mass of Sutra literature also is not without evidences pointing to the commercial connection of India with foreign countries by way of the sea. That these evidences are sufficiently convincing will probably be apparent from the following remarks of the well-known German authority, the late Professor Bühler: "References to sea voyages are also found in two of the most ancient *Dharma Sutras*. Baudhāyana, *Dh. S.* ii. 2. 2, forbids[2] them to the orthodox Brahmans, and prescribes a severe penance for a transgression of the prohibition, but he admits,[3] *Dh. S.* i. 2. 4, that such transgressions were common among the 'Northerners' or, strictly speaking, the Aryans

---

[1] ततः प्रवासितो विद्वान् विदुरेण नरस्तदा ।
पार्थानां दर्शयामास मनोमारुतगामिनीम् ॥
सर्व्ववातसहां नावं यन्त्रयुक्तां पताकिनीम् ।
शिवे भागीरथीतीरे नरैर्विस्रम्भिभिः कृताम् ॥

आदिपर्व्व ।

[2] "Now (follow the offences) causing loss of caste, (viz.) making voyages by sea." (Bühler's translation in *S.B.E.*)

[3] "Now (the customs peculiar) to the North are, to deal in wool, to drink rum, to sell animals that have teeth in the upper and in the lower jaws, to follow the trade of arms, to go to sea." (*Ibid.*)

living north of the author's home, the Dravidian districts. The forbidden practices mentioned in the same *Sutra* as customary among the Northerners, such as the traffic in wool and in animals with two rows of teeth (horses, mules, etc.), leave no doubt that the inhabitants of Western and North-Western India are meant. It follows as a matter of course that their trade was carried on with Western Asia. The same author,[1] *Dh. S.* i. 18. 14, and Gautama,[2] x. 33, fix also the duties payable by ship-owners to the king." The later *Smṛitis* also contain explicit references to sea-borne trade. *Manu* (iii. 158) declares a Brahman[3] who has gone to sea to be unworthy of entertainment at a *Srāddha*. In chapter viii. again of Manu's Code[4] there is an interesting sloka laying down the law that the rate

---

[1] "The duty on goods imported by sea is, after deducting a choice article, ten Panas in the hundred." (Bühler's translation in *S.B.E.*)

[2] "Hereby (the taxes payable by) those who support themselves by personal labour have been explained, and those payable by owners of ships and carts." (*Ibid.*)

[3] आगारदाही गरदः कुण्डाशी सोमविक्रयी ।
समुद्रयायी बन्दी च तैलिकः कूटकारकः ॥

["An incendiary, a prisoner, he who eats the food given by the son of an adulteress, a seller of *soma*, he who undertakes voyages by sea, a bard, an oilman, a suborner to perjury."]

[4] समुद्रयानकुशला देशकालार्थदर्शिनः ।
स्थापयन्ति तु यां वृद्धिं सा तत्राधिगमं प्रति ॥

["Whatever rate men fix, who are expert in sea voyages and able to calculate (the profit) according to the place, and the time, and the objects (carried), that (has legal force) in such cases with respect to the payment (to be made)."]

of interest on the money lent on bottomry is to be fixed by men well acquainted with sea voyages or journeys by land. In the same chapter there is another passage[1] which lays down the rule of fixing boat-hire in the case of a river journey and a sea voyage. But perhaps the most interesting passages in that important chapter are those which are found to lay down the rules regarding what may be called marine insurance. One of them holds the sailors collectively responsible for the damage caused by their fault to the goods of passengers, and the other absolves them from all responsibility if the damage is caused by an accident beyond human control.[2] Manu also mentions a

---

[1] दीर्घाध्वनि यथादेशं यथाकालं तरो भवेत् ।
नदीतीरेषु तद्विद्यात् समुद्रे नास्ति लक्षणम् ॥

["For a long passage the boat-hire must be proportioned to the places and times. Know that this (rule refers) to passages along the banks of rivers; at sea there is no settled (freight)."]

[2] The passages in question are:—

यन्नावि किंचिद्दाशानां विशीर्येतापराधतः ।
तद्दाशैरेव दातव्यं समागम्य स्वतोंऽशतः ॥
एष नौयायिनामुक्तो व्यवहारस्य निर्णयः ।
दाशापराधतस्तोये दैविके नास्ति निग्रहः ॥

(*Manu*, viii. 409. 9.)

["Whatever may be damaged in a boat by the fault of the boatmen, that shall be made good by the boatmen collectively (each paying) his share.

"This decision in suits (brought) by passengers (holds good only) in case the boatmen are culpably negligent on the water; in the case of (accident) caused by (the will of) the gods, no fine can be (inflicted on them)."]

particular caste of Hindus entrusted with the business of conducting trade, and upon them was enjoined the necessity of making themselves acquainted with the productions and requirements of other countries, with various dialects and languages, and also with whatever has direct or indirect reference to purchase or sale. In the *Yājñavalkya Sañhitā*[1] there is a passage which indicates that the Hindus were in the habit of making adventurous sea voyages in pursuit of gain.

The astronomical works also are full of passages that hint at the flourishing condition of Indian shipping and shipbuilding and the development of sea-borne trade. Thus the *Vṛihat Sañhitā* has several passages of this kind having an indirect bearing on shipping and maritime commerce. One of these indicates the existence of shippers and sailors as a class whose health is said to be influenced by the moon.[2] Another[3] mentions the stellar influences affecting the fortunes of traders,

---

[1] ये समुद्रगा वृद्ध्या धनं गृहीत्वा अधिकलाभार्थं प्राणधनविनाशशङ्कास्थानं समुद्रं गच्छन्ति ते विंशं शतकं मासि मासि दद्युः ।

[2] उन्नतमीषच्छृङ्गं नौसंस्थाने विशालता चोक्ता ।
नाविकपीड़ा तस्मिन् भवति शिवं सर्व्वलोकस्य ॥
(4. 8.)

[3] आश्विनयाम्यमूलान्युपमृद्नन् रेवतीश्च चन्द्रसुतः ।
पण्य भिषक् नौजीविक तुरगोपघात करः ॥
(7. 6.)

physicians, shippers, and the like. The third,[1] also, mentions a particular conjunction of stars similarly affecting merchants and sailors. The fourth passage[2] mentions the existence of a class of small shippers who probably are confined to inland navigation. The fifth[3] mentions the causes which bring about the sickness of passengers sailing in sea-going vessels on voyages, and of others. The last passage[4] I would cite here is that which recommends as the place for an auspicious sea-bath the seaport where there is a great flow of gold due to multitudes of merchantmen arriving in safety, after disposing of exports abroad, laden with treasure.

The *Purāṇas*[5] also furnish references to merchants engaged in sea-borne trade. The *Varāha*

---

[1] स्वातौ प्रभूतवृष्टिर्दूतवणिक् नाविकान् स्पृशत्यनयः ।
ऐन्द्राग्नेऽपि सुवृष्टिर्वणिजाञ्च भयं विजानीयात् ॥
(9. 31.)

[2] तुरग तुरगोपचारककविवैद्यामात्यहार्कजोऽश्वि गतः ।
याम्ये नर्तकवादकगेयज्ञ क्षुद्र नौ कृतिकान् ॥
(10. 3.)

[3] चित्रायां प्रमदाजनलेखक चित्रज्ञ चित्रभाण्डानि ।
स्वातौ मागधचरदूतसूत पोतप्लव नटाद्याः ॥
(10. 10.)

[4] अथवा समुद्रतीरे कुशलागतपोत सम्बाधे ।
धनविचुलीनजलचरसितबलमबलोकनोपान्ते ॥
(44. 12.)

[5] E.g. the *Vayu Purāṇa*, the *Mārkaṇḍeya Purāṇa*, and the *Bhāgavata Purāṇa*.

Purāṇa mentions a childless merchant named Gokarṇa who embarked on a voyage for trading purposes but was overtaken by a storm on the sea and nearly shipwrecked. The same *Purāṇa*[1] contains a passage which relates how a merchant embarked on a voyage in a sea-going vessel in quest of pearls with people who knew all about them. In the *Mārkaṇḍeya Purāṇa*[2] also there is a well-known passage repeated as *mantram* by thousands of Brahmans which refers as an illustration to the dangerous plight of the man sailing on the great ocean in a ship overtaken by a whirlwind.

But besides the religious works like the *Vedas*, the Epics, and the *Sutras* and *Purāṇas*, the secular works of Sanskrit poets and writers are also full of references to the use of the sea as the highway of commerce, to voyages, and naval fights. Thus in Kālidāsa's *Raghuvaṅsa* (canto 4, sloka 36) we find the defeat by Raghu of a strong naval

---

[1] पुनस्तत्रैव गमने वणिग् भावे मतिर्गता ।
समुद्रयाने रत्नानि महास्थौल्यानि साधुभिः ॥
रत्न परीक्षकैः सार्द्धमानायिष्ये बहूनि च ।
एवं निश्चित्य मनसा महासार्थपुरःसरः ।
समुद्रयायिभिर्लोकैः संविदं सूत्र्यनिर्गतः ॥
मुक्तेन सह संप्राप्तो महान्तं लवणार्णवम् ।
पोतारूढास्ततः सर्व्वे पोतवाहैरुपोषिता ॥

[2] मार्कण्डेयपुराणान्तर्गतदेवीमाहात्म्ये—
राज्ञा क्रुद्धेन चाज्ञप्तो वध्यो बन्धगतोऽपि वा ।
आघूर्णितो वा वातेन स्थितः पोते महार्णवे ॥

force with which the kings of Bengal attacked him, and his planting the pillars of victory on the isles formed in the midst of the River Ganges.[1] The *Raghuvaṅsa* also mentions the carrying even into Persia of the victorious arms of Raghu, though of course he reached Persia[2] by the land route. But this express reference to land route implies that the water route was well known. In Kālidāsa's *Sakuntalā* we have already noted the reference to China as the land of silk fabrics. The *Sakuntalā* also relates the story of a merchant named Dhanavṛiddhi whose immense wealth devolved to the king on the former's perishing at sea and leaving no heirs behind him. The popular drama of *Ratnāvalī*, which is usually attributed to King Harsha, relates the story[3] of the Ceylonese princess, daughter of King Vikramavāhu,

---

[1] वङ्गान् उत्खाय तरसा नेता नौसाधनोद्यतान् ।
निचखान जयस्तम्भं गङ्गास्रोतोऽन्तरेषु च ॥

["Having by his prowess uprooted the Vaṅgas (Bengalis) arrayed for battle with a naval force, that excellent leader (Raghu) posted pillars of victory on the isles formed in the midst of Gangā."]

[2] पारसीकान् ततो जेतुं प्रतस्थे स्थलवर्त्मना ।

[3] अन्यथा क्व सिद्धादेशजनितप्रत्ययप्रार्थितायाः सिंहलेश्वरदुहितुः समुद्रे यानभङ्गनिमग्नायाः फलकासादनम् । क्व च कौशाम्बीयेन वणिजा सिंहलेभ्यः प्रत्यागच्छता तदवस्थायाः संभावनम् ।

["Otherwise how was the attainment of a plank possible of the daughter of the king of Siṅhala, shipwrecked on the sea, with her desire kindled by the faith born of the words of saints? How also was she observed in that state by the merchant of Kausambi returning from Ceylon?"]

being shipwrecked in mid-ocean and brought thence by some merchants of the town of Kausambi. In the *Daśakumāracharita* of Dandin there is the story[1] of a merchant named Ratnodbhava who goes to an island called Kālayavaṇa, marries there a girl, but while returning home is shipwrecked; and another of Mitragupta,[2] who goes on board a Yavaṇa ship, and, losing his way, arrives at an isle different from his destination. The *S'iśupālavadha*[3] of the poet Māgha contains an interesting passage which mentions how S'rī Kṛishña, while going from Dvārakā to Hastināpura, beholds merchants coming from foreign countries in ships laden with merchandise and again exporting abroad Indian goods.

---

[1] ततः सोदरविलोकनकुतूहलेन रत्नोद्भवः कथञ्चिच्छ्वशुरमनुनीय चपललोचनयानया सह प्रवहणमारुह्य पुष्पपुरमभिप्रतस्थे। कल्लोलमालिकाभिहतः पोतः समुद्राम्भस्यमज्जत्।

[Then, anxious to see his brother, Ratnodbhava, with the permission of his father-in-law, started for Pushpapur (Patna) on board a ship with his wife, having her eyes rolling. The vessel sank in the water of the sea, being beaten by rolling waves.]

[2] अस्मिन्नेवक्षणेनैकनौकापरिवृतः कोऽपि मद्गुः अभ्यधावत्। अबिभयुर्यवनाः। तावदतिजवा नौकाः श्वान इव वराहमस्मत्पोतं पर्यरुत्सत।

[At this very moment a fleet of many ships was in pursuit. The Yavaṇas were afraid. Then like dogs attacking a boar the pursuing vessels very soon surrounded the ship.]

[3] विक्रीय दिश्यानि धनान्युरूणि द्वैप्यानसावुत्तमलाभभाजः।
तरीषु तत्रत्यमफल्गुभाण्डं सांयात्रिकानावपतोऽभ्यनन्दत्॥

[He (Sri Kṛishña) was glad to see merchants of distant islands, after realizing great profits from the sale of the products of many countries, reload their vessels with merchandise of Indian origin.]

In the vast Sanskrit literature of fables and fairy tales also there are many allusions to merchants and sea-borne trade. Thus the *Kathāsarit Sāgara* of the Kashmirian poet Somadeva bristles with references to sea voyages and intercourse with foreign countries. In the 9th book or *Lambaka*, 1st chapter or *Taraṅga*, there is the story of Prithvi Rāj going with an artist in a ship to the island of Muktipura; the 2nd chapter relates the voyages of a merchant and his wife to an island, and their separation after a shipwreck by storm; the 4th chapter describes the voyage of Samudrasura and another merchant to the Suvarṇa Island for commerce, and their shipwreck; the 6th chapter recounts the quest of his son by Chandrasvāmī, who goes to Ceylon and other islands in many a merchant's vessel for the purpose; and so on. The *Hitopadēśa* also mentions the story of Kandarpaketu, a merchant. In the *Hitopadēśa* a ship is described as a necessary requisite for a man to traverse the ocean, and a story is given of a certain merchant who, after having been twelve years on his voyage, at last returned home with a cargo of precious stones. In the *Nītiśataka* of Vartṛihari[1] there is a passage

[1] पोतो दुस्तर-वारिराशितरणे दीपोऽन्धकारागमे
निर्व्वाते व्यजनं मदान्धकरिणां दर्पोपशान्त्यै सृणिः ।
इत्थं तद् भुवि नास्ति यस्य विधिना नोपाय-चिन्ता कृता
मन्ये दुर्ज्जन-चित्तवृत्तिहरणे धातापि भग्नोद्यमः ।

which refers to ships as the means of crossing the illimitable expanse of water, even as lamps destroy darkness. The *Rāja-Taraṅginī*[1] contains a passage describing the misfortunes of a royal messenger on the sea.

Lastly, we may notice in this connection the frequent mention in ancient Sanskrit literature of pearls and references to pearl fishery as one of the important national industries of India, and especially in the land of the Tamils towards the south. It is hardly necessary to point out that pearls could not have been procured without the aid of adventurous mariners and boats that could breast the ocean wave and brave the perils of the deep. According to Varāhamihira, *Garuḍa Purāṇa*, and Bhoja, pearl-fishing was carried on in the whole of the Indian Ocean as far as the Persian Gulf, and its chief centres were off the coasts of Ceylon, Pāralaukika, Saurāshṭra, Tāmraparṇī, Pārasava, Kauvera, Pāndyavāṭaka, and Haimadesha. According to Agastya, the chief centres of Indian pearl-fishing were in the neighbourhood of Ceylon, Arabia, and Persia. Pearls were also artificially manufactured by Ceylonese craftsmen, but the Tamils were through-

---

[1] सान्धिविग्रहिकः सोऽथ गच्छन् पोतच्युतोऽम्बुधौ ।
प्राप पारं तिमिग्रासात्तिमिमुत्पाट्य निर्गतः ॥

[The royal messenger fell into the sea while proceeding on a vessel, and a whale devoured him ; but ripping open its belly, he came out and crossed the sea.]

out the most famous among Indians for pearl fishery, and they gave to the Gulf of Mannar the name of Salābhaṁ, "the sea of gain."

Thus Sanskrit literature in all its forms—such as the *Vedas*, the *Sutras*, the *Purāṇas*, poetry epic and dramatic, romance, etc.—is replete with references to the maritime trade of India, which prove that the ocean was freely used by the Indians in ancient times as the great highway of international commerce.

Further, the conclusions pointed to by these evidences from Sanskrit literature receive their confirmation again from the evidences furnished by the Buddhistic literature—the ancient historical works or the chronicles of Ceylon, the canonical books, and the *Jātakas* or Re-birth stories. The accounts of the Vijayan legends as set forth in the *Mahāwaṅso* and other works are full of references to the sea and sea-borne trade. According to the *Rājavalliya*, Prince Vijaya and his seven hundred followers were banished by the king Siṅhaba (Siṅhavāhu) of Beṅgal for the oppressions they practised upon his subjects, and they were put on board a ship and sent adrift, while their wives and children were placed in two other separate ships and sent away similarly. The ships started from a place near the city of Siṅhapura, and on their way touched at the port of Supara, which, according to Dr. Burgess, lay near the modern Bassein on the western coast of the Deccan. Vijaya landed in Ceylon "on the day that the successor of former Buddhas reclined in the arbour of the two delightful Sal-trees to attain Nirvāṇa," approaching the island from southwards, and became the founder of the "Great Dynasty." Vijaya then sent a present of precious stones to the king of Pandya, and caused to be brought a princess whom he took to wife, and also seven hundred women attendants whom his followers married. According to Turnour's *Mahāwaṅso*, the ship in which Vijaya's Pandyan bride was brought over to Ceylon was of a very large size, having the capacity to accommodate eighteen officers of state, seventy-five menial servants and a number of slaves, besides the princess herself and seven hundred other virgins who accompanied her. A period of interregnum followed after the death of Vijaya without issue till his nephew, "attended by thirty-two ministers, embarked from the city of Sagal," reached Ceylon, and assumed the reins of sovereignty. There are two further sea voyages [1] mentioned in this connection, the first undertaken by a princess who afterwards became the consort of Vijaya's nephew, and the second by her six brothers, both of which had the same starting-point in the city of Morapura on the Ganges, and the same destination,

---

[1] Upham's *Sacred and Historical Books of Ceylon*, i. 71; ii. 177. Turnour's *Mahāwaṅso*, 55.

viz. Ceylon, and the latter voyage, according to Turnour's *Mahāwaṅso*, occupied twelve days.

Next in importance to the Vijayan legends,[1] so far as sea-borne trade is concerned, are the legends of Punna, a merchant of Supparaka, who carried on a large trade, in partnership with his younger brother Chula Punna, with the distant region of Northern Kosala. At Srāvasti he heard Buddha preach, and became his disciple, and afterwards induced his former mercantile associates of Supparaka to erect a Vihāra with a portion of the red-sanders timber which Chula Punna and his three hundred associate merchants brought home on one of their sea voyages. The ship in which they made their trading voyage was of so large a size that besides accommodating over three hundred merchants there was room left for the cargo of that timber which they brought home. The legends next requiring notice in this connection are those of the two Burmese[2] merchant brothers Tapoosa and Palekat, who crossed the Bay of Bengal in a ship that conveyed full five hundred cartloads of their own goods, which they landed at Adzeitta, a port in Kalinga in the northern section of the eastern coast, on their way to Suvama in Magadha. Again, in the legend of the conveyance of the Tooth-relic, as

---

[1] Hardy, *Manual of Buddhism*, 56, 57, and 60.

[2] Bishop Bigandet's *Life of Godama*, 101.

related in the *Dāthādhātuwańso*, there is mention of the voyage of Dantakumara conveying the relic from Dantapura to Ceylon. The voyage was performed in one of those ships which carried on a regular and ceaseless traffic between the port of Tamralipta in Bengal and the island of Ceylon.

The Tibetan legend of the Sinhalese princess Ratnāvalī may also be mentioned, which tells of the voyage of the merchants of Srāvasti who were driven down the Bay of Bengal by contrary winds, but who subsequently completed their voyage to Ceylon and back. Again, in one of the Chinese legends of the lion-prince Sińhala,[1] it is related how the boat in which the daughter of the Lion was cast away was driven by the winds westwards into the Persian Gulf, where she landed and founded a colony "in the country of the Western women." The tradition embodied in the *Dīpavańsa* version of the legend[2] makes her land on an island which was afterwards called the "Kingdom of Women." As the Rev. T. Foulkes[3] remarks, "underneath the legendary matter we may here trace the existence of a sea route between India and the Persian coasts in the days of Buddha."

---

1 *Si-yu-ki*, ii. 246.

2 *Si-yu-ki*, xiii. 55.

3 *Indian Antiquary*, 1879.

Among the *Pitakas*, the *Vinaya* mentions a Hindu merchant named Poorna who made six sea voyages, and in the seventh voyage he was in the company of some Buddhist citizens of Sravasti and was converted by them to Buddhism. The *Sutta Pitaka* contains also several allusions to voyages in distant seas far remote from land. In the *Sañyutta Nikaya* (3, p. 115, 5. 51) and in the *Añguttara* (4. 127) there are interesting passages which mention voyages, lasting for six months, made in ships (*nāva*, which means boats) which could be drawn up on shore in the winter. Very interesting and conclusive evidence is supplied by a passage in the *Digha Nikaya* (1.. 222) which distinctly mentions sea voyages out of sight of land. It describes how merchants carrying on sea-borne trade would take with them in their sea-going vessels certain birds of strong wing which, when the vessels were out of sight of land, would be let loose and used to indicate in which direction the land lay. If the shore were not near or within easy reach, the birds would return to the ships after flying in all directions to get to land, but if there were land within a few miles the birds would not return.

Some very definite and convincing allusions to sea voyages and sea-borne trade are also contained in the vast body of Buddhist literature known as the *Jātakas*, which are generally taken to relate themselves to a period of one thousand years beginning from 500 B.C. The *Baveru-Jātaka*[1] without doubt points to the existence of commercial intercourse between India and Babylon in pre-Asokan days. The full significance of this important *Jātaka* is thus expressed by the late Professor Bühler: "The now well-known *Baveru-Jātaka*, to which Professor Minayef first drew attention, narrates that Hindu merchants exported peacocks to Baveru. The identification of Baveru with Babiru or Babylon is not doubtful," and considering the "age of the materials of the *Jātakas*, the story indicates that the Vanias of Western India undertook trading voyages to the shores of the Persian Gulf and of its rivers in the 5th, perhaps even in the 6th century B.C. just as in our days. This trade very probably existed already in much earlier times, for the *Jātakas* contain several other stories, describing voyages to distant lands and perilous adventures by sea, in which the names of the very ancient Western ports of Surparaka-Supara and Bharukaccha-Broach are occasionally mentioned." The *Samudda-Vanija-Jātaka*[2] tells the story of the village[3] of wood-wrights who, failing to deliver the goods[4] (furniture,

---

[1] *Jataka* iii., no. 339, in the Cambridge Edition.

[2] *Jataka* iv. 159, no. 466.

[3] "There stood near Benares a great town of carpenters containing a thousand families."—*Ibid.*

[4] "The carpenters from this town used to profess that they would make a bed or a chair or a house."—*Ibid.*

etc.) for which they had been paid in advance, built a ship secretly, embarked their families, and emigrated down the Ganges and out to an island over-sea.[1] The *Vālahassa-Jātaka* (*Jāt.* ii. 128, no. 196) mentions[2] five hundred dealers[3] who were fellow passengers on an ill-fated ship. The *Supparaka-Jātaka*[4] (*Jāt.* iv. 138–142) records the perilous adventures on the sea undergone by a company of seven hundred merchants[5] who sailed from the seaport town of Bharukaccha[6] in a vessel under the pilotage of a blind but accomplished mariner.[7] The *Mahājanaka-Jātaka* (*Jāt.* vi. 32–35, no. 539)

---

[1] "There they sailed at the wind's will until they reached an island that lay in the midst of the sea."—*Ibid.*

[2] The *Valahassa-Jātaka* relates how "some shipwrecked mariners escaped from a city of goblins by the aid of a flying horse."—*Ibid.*

[3] "Now it happened that five hundred shipwrecked traders were cast ashore near the city of these sea-goblins."—*Ibid.*

[4] "The story mentions how a blind mariner was made the king's assessor and valuer, and how he was pilot to a vessel which traversed the perilous seas of Fairyland."—*Ibid.*

[5] "It happened that some merchants had got ready a ship and were casting about for a skipper. . . . Now there were seven hundred souls aboard the ship."—*Ibid.*

[6] "There was a seaport town named Bharukacch or Marsh of Bharu. At that time the Buddhisatta was born into the family of a master mariner there. . . . They gave him the name of Supparaka Kumara. . . . Afterwards, when his father died, he became the head of his mariners. . . . With him aboard no ship ever came to harm."—*Ibid.*

[7] "Four months the vessel had been voyaging in far-distant regions; and now, as though endowed with supernatural powers, it returned in one single day to the seaport town of Bharukacch."—*Ibid.*

recounts the adventures[1] of a prince who, with other traders, is represented as setting out[2] from Champa with export goods[3] for Suvannabhumi on the same ship which is wrecked in mid-ocean—Suvannabhumi is "probably either Burma or the 'Golden Chersonese' or the whole Farther-Indian coast"—and this *Jātaka* also shows that the Ganges was navigable right away to the sea from Champa or modern Bhagalpur. The *Sāṅkha-Jātaka* (*Jāt.* vi. 15–17, no. 442) tells the story of a Brahman given to charity who sails in a ship for the Gold Country in quest of riches by which he can replenish the store[4] his philanthropy was exhausting. He was a native of Benares, and gave away daily in

---

[1] The following is a brief summary of its story: A prince suspects his brother, without reason, rebels against him, and kills him. The king's consort, being with child, flees from the city. Her son is brought up without knowledge of his father, but when he learns the truth goes to sea on a merchant venture. He is wrecked, and a goddess brings him to his father's kingdom, where, after answering some difficult questions, he marries the daughter of the usurper. By-and-bye he becomes an ascetic, and is followed by his wife. (Cambridge edition of the *Jātakas.*)

[2] "Having got together his stock-in-trade (viz. store of pearls, jewels, and diamonds) he put it on board a ship with some merchants bound for Suvannabhumi, and bade his mother farewell, telling her that he was sailing for that country."—*Ibid.*

[3] "There were seven caravans with their beasts embarked on board. In seven days the ship made seven hundred leagues, but having gone too violently in its course it could not hold out."—*Ibid.*

[4] "One day he thought to himself, 'My store of wealth once gone I shall have nothing to give. While it is still unexhausted I will take ship, and sail for the Gold Country, whence I will bring back wealth. So he caused a ship to be built, filled it with merchandise, and, bidding farewell to his wife and child, set his face towards the seaport, and at mid-day he departed."—*Ibid.*

alms 600,000 pieces of money. His ship, however, sprang a leak[1] in mid-ocean, but he is miraculously saved by a kind fairy in a magic ship[2] filled with the seven treasures of gold, silver, pearls, gems, cats'-eyes, diamonds, and coral. The *Sussondi-Jātaka* (*Jāt.* iii. 188, no. 360) mentions the voyage of certain merchants of Bharukaccha for the Golden Land,[3] from which, as also from other *Jātakas* such as the *Mahājanaka-Jātaka*, it is evident that besides Ceylon, Suvannabhumi or Burma was another commercial objective of traders coasting around India from western seaports such as Bharukaccha. Lastly, there are several other *Jātakas* in which we are told explicitly of a successful, if sporadic, deal in birds between Babylon and Benares, and of horses[4]

[1] "When they were come to the high seas, on the seventh day the ship sprang a leak, and they could not bale the water clear."—*Ibid.*

[2] The following contains a full description of the ship: "The deity, well pleased at hearing these words, caused a ship to appear made of the seven things of price; in length it was 800 cubits, 20 fathoms in depth; it had three masts made of sapphire, cordage of gold, silver sails, and of gold also were the oars and the rudders."—*Ibid.*

[3] "At that time certain merchants of Bharukaccha were setting sail for the Golden Land."—*Ibid.*

[4] *Jātaka* i. 124, or *Tandulanali-Jātaka*, no. 5, which tells the story of an incompetent valuer declaring five hundred horses worth a measure of rice, which measure of rice in turn he is led to declare worth all Benares, contains a passage of which the following is the English translation: "At that time there arrived from the North Country a horse-dealer with five hundred horses." Similarly, *Jātaka* ii. 31, *Suhanu-Jātaka*, no. 158, has the following: "Some horse-dealers from the North Country brought down five hundred horses." Again, *Jātaka* ii. 287, or *Kundaka-Kucchi-Sindhava-Jātaka*,

imported by hundreds from the North and from Sindh.[1]

The conclusions regarding the state of Indian trade to which these various hints in the *Jātakas* point may be thus summed up in the words of Mrs. Rhys Davids :—

> Communication both inland and foreign was of course effected by caravans and water. The caravans are described as consisting of five hundred carts drawn by oxen. They go both east and west from Benares and Patna as centres. The objective was probably the ports on the west coast, those on the sea-board of Sobira (the Sophir (Ophir) of the Septuagint) in the Gulf of Cutch or Bharukaccha. From here there was interchange by sea with Baveru (Babylon) and probably Arabia, Phoenicia, and Egypt. . . . Westward merchants are often mentioned as taking ships from Benares, or lower down at Champa, dropping down the great river, and either coasting to Ceylon or adventuring many days without sight of land to Suvannabhumi (Chryse Chersonesus, or possibly inclusive of all the coast of Farther India).[2]

---

no. 254, mentions how the "Boddhisatta was born into a trader's family in the Northern Province; and five hundred people of that country, horse-dealers, used to convey horses to Benares and sell them there."

[1] *Jātaka* i. 178, or *Bhojajanuya-Jātaka*, no. 23, mentions how "Boddhisatta came to life as a thoroughbred Sindh horse." Similarly, *Jātaka* i. 181, or the *Ajanna-Jātaka*, no. 24, refers to a warrior who fought from a chariot to which were harnessed two Sindh horses.

[2] *Economic Journal* and *J.R.A.S.* for 1901.

BOOK I.—PART II.

The History of Indian Maritime Activity.

BOOK I.—PART II.

CHAPTER I.

The Pre-Mauryan Period.

Both Brahminical and Buddhistic texts are thus replete with references to the sea-borne trade of India that directly and indirectly demonstrate the existence and development of a national shipping and shipbuilding. It is now necessary to narrate the facts of that trade, and for this we shall have to draw upon all sorts of evidence, literary, inscriptional, and numismatic, and both Indian and foreign. For India alone has not the monopoly of these evidences; and if she really had commercial connection with the outside world it is natural, and in fact necessary, that they be also supplied by those countries with which she carried on her intercourse, thus confirming those conclusions that are reached by a study of the purely Indian evidences. And so do we find, as a matter of fact, in various foreign works abundant allusions to India's commerce, arts, and manufactures, indicating the glorious position she once occupied and for long maintained as the Queen of the Eastern Seas.

Indeed, all the evidences available will clearly show that for full thirty centuries India stood out as the very heart of the commercial world, cultivating trade relations successively with the Phoenicians, Jews, Assyrians, Greeks, Egyptians, and Romans in ancient times, and Turks, Venetians, Portuguese, Dutch, and English in modern times. A genial climate and a fertile soil, coupled with the industry and frugality of the Indian people, rendered them virtually independent of foreign nations in respect of the necessaries of life, while their secondary wants were few. Of the latter, tin, lead, glass, amber, steel for arms, and perhaps coral and to a small extent medicinal drugs, were all that India had need to import from Europe and Western Asia, while to Arabia she was indebted for the supply of frankincense used in her temples. On the other hand, India provided Europe with wool from the fleeces of the sheep bred on her north-western mountain ranges, famous since the days of Alexander the Great; with onyx, chalcedony, lapis-lazuli, and jasper, then esteemed as precious stones; with a resinous gum, furs, assafoetida, and musk; with embroidered woollen fabrics and coloured carpets which were as highly prized in Babylon and Rome as their modern reproductions are in London and Paris at the present day. But the most valuable of the exports of India was silk, which, under the Persian Empire, is said to have been exchanged by weight with gold. It was manufactured in India, as well as obtained for re-export from China. Next to silk in value were cotton cloths ranging from coarse canvas and calicoes to muslins of the finest texture. India also supplied foreign countries with oils, brassware, a liquid preparation of the sugar-cane, salt, drugs, dyes, and aromatics, while she had also a monopoly in the matter of the supply of pepper, cinnamon, and other edible spices, which were in great request throughout Europe.

Through ages India thus occupied a unique position in the commercial world as the main supplier of the world's luxuries. As a consequence she throughout had the balance of trade clearly in her favour, a balance which could only be settled by the export of treasure from European and other countries that were commercially indebted to her. For India desired nothing which foreigners could give her but the precious metals. Thus has she been for many centuries the final depository of a large portion of the metallic wealth of the world. Her supply of gold she obtained not as did Europe from America in the 16th century by conquest or rapine, but by the more natural and peaceful method of commerce, " by the exchange of such of her productions as among the Indians were superfluities but were at the same time not only highly prized by the nations of Western Asia, Egypt, and Europe, but were obtainable from no other quarter except India, or from the farther East by means of the Indian trade."[1] It was this flow or "*drain" of gold into India* that so far back as the 1st century A.D. was the cause of alarm and regret to Pliny, who calculated that fully a hundred million sesterces, equivalent, according to Delmar, to £70,000 of modern English money, were withdrawn annually from the Roman Empire to purchase useless Oriental products such as perfumes, unguents, and personal ornaments.[2] It was probably also the same flow of gold into India from outside that even earlier still, in the 5th century B.C., at least partially enabled the Indian satrapy of Darius, naturally the richest and most populous part of his empire (including as much of Afghanistan, Kashmir, and the Punjab as the Persian monarchs could keep in subjection), to pay him "the enormous tribute of 360 Euboic talents of gold-dust or 185 hundredweights, worth fully a million sterling, and constituting about one-third of the total bullion revenue of the Asiatic provinces."[3]

We shall now enter upon a relation of the facts of this trade which served to create "the wealth of Ind," a brief survey of its course which undoubtedly is an important, though neglected, aspect

---

[1] C. Daniell, F.S.S., I.C.S., *Industrial Competition of Asia*, p. 225.

[2] Pliny, *Natural History*, xii. 18. See also Mommsen's *Provinces of the Roman Empire*, vol. ii., 299–300.

[3] *Herodotus*, iii. (V. A. Smith's *Early History of India*, New Edition, p. 34).

of Indian history, the story of her old, abounding international life.

The antiquity of this trade will be evident from the fact that it is foreshadowed even in the *Ṛig-Veda*, one of the oldest literary records of humanity, which, as I have already shown, speaks in many places of ships and merchants sailing out into the open main for the sake of riches, braving the perils of the deep, "where there is no support, nothing to rest upon or cling to." India thus began her sea-borne trade with the very beginning of recorded time, and the trade of the *Ṛig-Veda* was very probably carried on with countries on the west like Chaldaea, Babylon, and Egypt. I do not feel myself competent to deal with this subject of India's prehistoric trade relations; Egyptologists or Assyriologists alone can do full justice to it. I can but briefly refer to some of the conclusions reached in regard to this subject and the evidences on which they are based. According to Dr. Sayce,[1] the famous Assyriologist, the commerce by sea between India and Babylon must have been carried on as early as about 3000 B.C., when Ur Bagas, the first king of United Babylonia, ruled in Ur of the Chaldees. This is proved by the finding of Indian teak in the ruins of Ur. Mr. Hewitt is of opinion

[1] See his *Hibbert Lectures* for 1887 on the Origin and Growth of Religion among the Babylonians.

that this wood must have been sent by sea from some port on the Malabar coast, for it is only there that teak grew near enough to the sea to be exported with profit in those early times. Again, Dr. Sayce points to the use of the word *sindhu* for muslin in an old Babylonian list of clothes as the clearest proof "that there was trade between Babylonia and people who spoke an Aryan dialect and lived in the country watered by the Indus." This trade must have been sea-borne, and the muslin must have been brought by sea, for, as Mr. Hewitt points out, if Zend-speaking traders had brought it by land they would have called the country by the Zend name, Hindhu, altering the *s* into an *h*.[1] These conclusions of Dr. Sayce and Mr. Hewitt regarding the extreme antiquity of the Indian maritime trade with Babylon are not, however, accepted by all scholars. Mr. J. Kennedy,[2] for instance, in a learned article on the subject, says that he "can find no archaeological or literary evidence for a maritime trade between India and Babylon prior to the 7th century B.C. . . . but for the 6th century B.C. direct evidence is forthcoming." This direct evidence, which is so very interesting, may be thus presented after him:—(1) Mr. Rassam found a beam of Indian cedar in

---

[1] *J.R.A.S.*, 1888, p. 337. Mr. Hewitt, late Commissioner of Chota Nagpur, is the author of many works on primitive history.

[2] See *J.R.A.S.*, 1898, on the Early Commerce between India and Babylon.

the palace of Nebuchadnezzar (604–562 B.C.) at Birs Nimrud, part of which is now exhibited in the British Museum. (2) In the second storey of the Temple of the Moon-god at Ur, rebuilt by Nebuchadnezzar and Nabonidus (555–538 B.C.) Mr. Taylor found "two rough logs of wood, apparently teak, which ran across the whole breadth of the shaft," and Mr. Rassam thus says of it in a letter: "Most probably the block of wood which Taylor discovered was Indian cedar like the beam I discovered in the palace of Nebuchadnezzar. There is no doubt that this wood was imported into Babylonia from India." (3) The *Baveru-Jātaka*, as we have already seen, relates the adventures of certain Indian merchants who took the first peacock by sea to Babylon. Mr. Kennedy remarks, "the *Jātaka* itself may go back to 400 B.C., but the folks-tale on which it is based must be much older." We have already cited the opinion on this *Jātaka* of the late Professor Bühler, according to whom, if the age of the materials of the *Jātakas* be considered, "the story indicates that the Vanias of Western India undertook trading voyages to the shores of the Persian Gulf or its rivers in the 5th, perhaps even in the 6th century B.C., just as in our days. This trade very probably existed already in much earlier times; for the *Jātakas* contain several other stories, describing voyages to distant lands and perilous adventures by sea, in which the names of the very ancient Western ports of Surparaka-Supara and Bharukaccha-Broach are occasionally mentioned."[1] We may also note in this connection that in the *Digha Nikaya* (I. 222) of Sutta-Pitaka, the date of which has been placed by Mr. Rhys Davids[2] in the 5th century B.C., there is an explicit reference to "ocean-going ships out of sight of land." (4) Certain Indian commodities, e.g. rice, peacocks, sandal-wood, were known to the Greeks and others under their Indian names in the 5th century B.C. "It follows that they were imported from the west coast of India into Babylon directly by sea; and this conclusion is borne out by the statements of the *Baveru-Jātaka*. And we must further conclude that they were first imported into Babylon in the 6th century B.C., not only because direct intercourse between Babylon and India practically came to an end after 480 B.C., but because rice and peacocks must have reached Greece at the latest in 460 or 470 B.C. in order to become common at Athens in 430 B.C." After this review of the evidence Mr. Kennedy puts forward the following conclusion: "The evidence warrants us in the belief that maritime commerce between India and Babylon flourished in the 7th and 6th, but more especially in the 6th, centuries B.C. It was

[1] *Origin of the Indian Brahma Alphabet*, p. 84.

[2] See *J.R.A.S.*, April, 1899, p. 482.

chiefly in the hands of Dravidians, although Âryans had a share in it; and as Indian traders settled afterwards in Arabia and on the east coast of Africa, and as we find them settling at this very time on the coast of China, we cannot doubt that they had their settlements in Babylon also." And he further remarks: "The history of the trade between Babylon and India suggests one remark: the normal trade route from the Persian Gulf to India can never have been along the inhospitable shores of Gedrosia."

Mr. Rhys Davids,[1] who has also dealt with this subject, has thus stated his conclusions:—(1) Sea-going merchants, availing themselves of the monsoons, were in the habit, at the beginning of the 7th (and perhaps at the end of the 8th) century B.C., of trading from ports on the south-west coast of India (Sovira at first, afterwards Supparaka and Bharukaccha) to Babylon, then a great mercantile emporium. (2) These merchants were mostly Dravidians, not Aryans. Such Indian names of the goods imported as were adopted in the West (Solomon's ivory, apes, and peacocks, for instance, and the word "rice") were adaptations not of Sanskrit or Pali, but of Tamil words.

The same view of this Indian trade with the West has been held by Mr. A. M. T. Jackson,

[1] *Buddhist India*, p. 116.

I.C.S.[1] According to him, "the Buddhist *Jatakas*[2] and some of the Sanskrit law-books[3] tell us that ships from Bhroach and Supara traded with Babylon (Baveru) from the 8th to the 6th century B.C."

There have been also other scholars who are disposed to view this maritime commerce of India with the West as of very great antiquity. According to Lenormant, the bas-reliefs of the temple of Deir-el-Bahari at Thebes represent the conquest of the land of Pun under Hatasu. "In the abundant booty loading the vessel of Pharaoh for conveyance to the land of Egypt appear a great many Indian animals and products not indigenous to the soil of Yemen—elephants' teeth, gold, precious stones, sandal-wood, and monkeys." Again, "The labours of Von Bohlen (*Das alte Indien*, vol. i., p. 42), confirming those of Heeren, and in their turn confirmed by those of Lassen (*Ind. Alt.*, vol. ii., p. 580), have established the existence of a maritime commerce between India and Arabia from the very earliest period of humanity."[4] The principal commodities imported from India were gold, precious stones, ivory, etc.

---

[1] *Bombay City Gazetteer*, vol. ii., ch. vi., p. 3.

[2] Nos. 339 and 463 (Fausboll).

[3] *S.B.E.*, ii. 228; xiv. 146, 200, 217.

[4] *Hist. Anc. del Orient*, English edition, vol. ii., pp. 299, 301, quoted in *I.A.*, vol. xiii., p. 228.

Further, according to Wilkinson,[1] the presence of indigo, tamarind-wood, and other Indian products has been detected in the tombs of Egypt, and Lassen also has pointed out that the Egyptians dyed cloth with indigo and wrapped their mummies in Indian muslin.

Lastly, this early maritime commerce of India, first vaguely hinted at in the *Ṛig-Veda*, and proved by the evidence of Egyptian and Assyrian archaeology, is further supposed by many competent authorities to be alluded to in several places in the Bible itself. "Even in the Mosaic period (1491–1450 B.C.) precious stones which were to a great extent a speciality of India and the neighbouring countries appear to have been well known and were already highly valued. It is probable that some of the stones in the breast-plate of the high priest may have come from the far East."[2] In the Book of Genesis[3] there is mention of a company of traders with their camels bearing spicery, balm, and myrrh, going to Egypt. In the days of Solomon (about 1015 B.C.) there could be supplied from India alone

---

[1] *Ancient Egyptians*, ii. 237, quoted by Delmar, Director of the Bureau of Statistics, U.S.A.

[2] Professor V. Ball, M.A., F.R.S., F.G.S., in his highly valuable article on "A Geologist's Contribution to the History of Ancient India," in the *I.A.* for August, 1884.

[3] Gen. xxxvii. 25: "Behold, a company of Ishmeelites came from Gilead with their camels bearing spicery and balm and myrrh, going to carry it down to Egypt."

the ivory, garments, armour, spices, and peacocks which found customers in ancient Syria. In the Book of 1 Kings it is stated[1] how the ships of Solomon came to Ophir and fetched from thence gold, plenty of almug trees, precious stones, and the like. In the Book of Ezekiel, which dwells on the commerce of Tyre, there are mentioned commodities which are undoubtedly of Indian origin.[2] Thus the ivory and ebony included in them are characteristic Indian products and were recognized as such by classical writers like Megasthenes,[3] Theophrastus,[4] and Virgil.[5] Besides, another proof that the Bible really refers to the foreign trade of India may be found in the fact that there have been discovered some old Dravidian words in the Hebrew text of the Books of Kings and Chronicles of the Old

---

[1] 1 Kings ix. 26, 27, 28: "And King Solomon made a navy of ships in Ezion-geber, which is beside Eloth, on the shore of the Red Sea . . . And Hiram sent in the navy his servants, shipmen that had knowledge of the sea, with the servants of Solomon. And they came to Ophir, and fetched from thence gold, four hundred and twenty talents, and brought it to King Solomon." 1 Kings x. 11: "And the navy also of Hiram, that brought gold from Ophir, brought in from Ophir great plenty of almug trees and precious stones."

[2] Ezekiel xxvii. 24: "These were thy merchants in all sorts of things, in blue clothes, and broidered work, and in chests of rich apparel, bound with cords." *Ibid.* 15: "They brought thee for a present horns of ivory and ebony."

[3] *Strabo*, xv. 37: "Ebony grows there."

[4] *History of Plants*, iv. 4, 6, quoted by McCrindle.

[5] *Georg.* i. 57: "India produces ivory." The *Periplus* also mentions logs of ebony exported from Barygaza-Broach.

Testament, where there is given the list of the articles of merchandise brought from Tarshish or Ophir in Solomon's ships "about 1000 B.C." Thus the word for "peacock" in the Hebrew text is *tuki* in Kings, *tuki* in Chronicles, while "the ancient, poetical, purely Tamil-Malayalam name of the peacock is *tokei*, the bird with the (splendid) tail."[1] Again, the Hebrew words *ahalim* or *ahaloth* for the fragrant wood called "aloes" in Proverbs vii. 17, etc., is derived from the Tamil-Malayalam form of the word *aghil*.

Without dwelling at any further length on the meaning of these Biblical allusions, I quote below the following interpretation put upon them by the learned bishop Dr. Caldwell, in his monumental work, *A Comparative Grammar of the Dravidian Languages*:—

> It seems probable that Aryan merchants from the mouth of the Indus must have accompanied the Phoenicians and Solomon's servants in their voyages down the Malabar coast towards Ophir (wherever Ophir may have been) or at least have taken part in the trade. . . . It appears certain from notices contained in the *Vedas* that the Aryans of the age of Solomon practised foreign trade in ocean-going vessels, but it remains uncertain to what parts their ships sailed.[2]

Bishop Caldwell's opinion is further supported by another erudite clergyman and scholar, the Rev.

---

[1] Dr. Caldwell, in his *Grammar of the Dravidian Languages*, p. 91. We may remember also in this connection the well-known reference in the *Baveru-Jātaka* to voyages made by Indian merchants to Babylon, in the second of which they took thither the first peacock for sale.

[2] *Grammar of the Dravidian Languages*, p. 122.

T. Foulkes,[1] who, in a very learned essay, comes to the same conclusion, and says :—

> The fact is now scarcely to be doubted that the rich Oriental merchandise of the days of King Hiram and King Solomon had its starting-place in the seaports of the Dakhan; and that with a very high degree of probability some of the most esteemed of the spices which were carried into Egypt by the Midianitish merchants of Genesis xxxvii. 25, 28, and by the sons of the patriarch Jacob (Gen. xliii. 11), had been cultivated in the spice-gardens of the Dakhan.

Thus the first trade of India of which there is any record was with Western Asia and Palestine. King Solomon tried to appropriate a share of this trade for the Jewish people by creating facilities for his Eastern traders both on land and sea routes. On the land route he built as resting-places for caravans the cities of Tadmor (Palmyra), Baalbec (Heliopolis), and Hamath (Epiphania), and his foresight in protecting these caravan routes bore fruit in the great trading centres of Mesopotamia, viz. Babylon, Ctesiphon, Seleucia, and Ossis, which all flourished for a long time on the profits of their commerce with the East. The Jewish monarch was also equally interested in the sea-borne trade of the East. His fleets made periodical voyages to and from the head of the Red Sea and the ports in the Persian Gulf, and we know from Holy Writ that " Ezion-geber, which is beside Eloth on the shore of the Red Sea in the land of Edom," was the

[1] *The Indian Antiquary*, vol. viii.

Syrian port for the arrival and departure of the fleets sent on these voyages. Their cargoes were carried by caravans to Petra and distributed some to Egypt and others to Rhinocolura, a port of the Mediterranean, for transhipment to Europe. The Phoenicians also took an active part in this trade, with Tyre as their headquarters. After the conquest of Tyre by Alexander the Great, and the foundation of Alexandria, the Egyptians came into the field, and after the successive decline of the Jewish, Phoenician, and Persian powers in Western Asia, they retained with the Arabians a monopoly of this commerce for about 900 years between Alexander's death and the conquest of Egypt by the Musalmans in the year 640 A.D.

We have now dealt with the foreign trade of India in the age of the Bible, and proceed to consider the notices left by the Greek writers of this period of the international intercourse of India. The earliest, probably, is that of Herodotus (450 B.C.), the father of history, whose reference to the Indian contingent[1] of Xerxes' army, clad in cotton garments and armed with cane bows and iron-tipped[2] cane arrows, is well known. Herodotus also speaks

---

[1] *Herodotus*, vii. 65, viii. 13, ix. 91. V. A. Smith remarks: "The archers from India formed a valuable element in the army of Xerxes, and shared the defeat of Mardonius at Plataea."

[2] *Cf.* V. Smith, *Early History of India*, p. 35: "The fact that the Indian troops used iron in 480 B.C. is worth noting."

of the inclusion of a part of India as the twentieth satrapy of the Emperor Darius,[1] a fact which in the opinion of scholars accounts for the traces of Persian influence[2] on old Indian art, architecture, and administrative methods. Among Indian products Herodotus noted the wool which certain wild trees bear instead of fruit, "that in beauty and quality excels that of sheep,"[3] of which Indians make their clothing.

Herodotus also gives us some insight into the nature and extent of certain Indian mineral productions. Babylon obtained precious stones and dogs (probably Tibetan mastiffs) from India.[4] In the enumeration of the nations and tribes which paid tribute to the Persian monarch Darius, the Indians alone, we are told, paid in gold, all the others paying in silver. The amount of this gold was 360 Euboic talents, equivalent to £1,290,000. Herodotus also pointedly speaks of India as being "rich in gold,"[5] and he relates the famous and widespread fable of the gold-digging ants, which has been shown by Sir Henry Robinson and Dr. Schiern[6]

---

[1] *Herodotus*, iii.

[2] See Smith's *Early History of India*, pp. 137, 153, 225, for an account of this Persian influence.

[3] *Herodotus*, iii. 106, in McCrindle's *Ancient India as Described in Classical Literature.*

[4] *Ibid.*, i. 192.

[5] *Ibid.*, iii. 106.

[6] *I.A.*, vol. iv., pp. 225 ff.

to have originated in the peculiar customs of the Tibetan gold-miners; and the name "ant gold" was possibly first given to the fragments of gold-dust brought from Tibet on account of their shape and size. The "horns of the gold-digging ants" mentioned by Pliny and others have been supposed to be simply samples of the ordinary pickaxes used by miners, which in Ladakh and Tibet were made of the horns of wild sheep, mounted on handles of wood. Herodotus may also have meant the gold-diggers of the desert of Gobi, who were in the habit of excavating gold from beneath the earth, and from them Indian traders of the Punjab neighbourhood could obtain their supply of gold. The portion of India conquered by Darius was situated chiefly to the north-west of the Indus, and, according to the authoritative testimony of Professor V. Ball, F.R.S., the eminent geologist, "the Indus itself, as well as some of its tributaries, is known to be auriferous." Professor Ball also rejects the view held by Lassen, Heeren, and many others that gold (and silver) was not indigenous to India, but imported from abroad, e.g. from Tibet, Burma, or even Africa;[1] for as he points out, "our most recent knowledge of India affords evidence that the amount of gold derived from indigenous sources must have been very considerable before the alluvial deposits were exhausted of their gold."

---

[1] *Asiatic Nations* (Bohn's ed.), vol. ii., p. 32.

The further remarks of Professor Ball in this connection are worth quoting in full:—

> When it is remembered that about 80 per cent. of the gold raised throughout the world is from alluvial washings, and when this fact is considered in connection with the reflection that wide tracts in Australia and America, formerly richly productive, are now deserted, being covered with exhausted tailings, it can be conceived how these regions in India—and there are very many of them—which are known to be auriferous, may, in the lapse of time, after yielding large supplies of gold, have become too exhausted to be of much present consideration. More than this, however, recent explorations have confirmed the fact, often previously asserted, that in Southern India there are indications of extended mining operations having been carried on there.
>
> Evidence exists of the most conclusive kind of large quantities of gold having been amassed by Indian monarchs, who accepted a revenue in gold-dust only from certain sections of their subjects, who were consequently compelled to spend several months of every year washing for it in the rivers.[1]

In Ctesias' *Indica* (400 B.C.), the earliest Greek treatise on India, is to be found, among other things, the existence of a really Dravidian word which Ctesias used for cinnamon.[2] The word used by Ctesias is *karpion*, which Dr. Caldwell derives from the Tamil-Malayalam word *karuppa* or *karppu*, to which is akin the Sanskrit word *karpura* "camphor."[3]

---

[1] *I.A.*, August, 1884.

[2] *Ctesias*, translated by McCrindle, p. 29. His *Indica* embodies the information he had gathered about India, "partly from the reports of Persian officials who had visited that country on the King's service, and partly also perhaps from the reports of Indians themselves who in those days were occasionally to be seen at the Persian Court, whither they resorted either as merchants or as envoys bringing presents and tribute from the princes of Northern India, which was then subject to Persian rule." (McCrindle's *Ctesias*, Introduction, p. 3.)

[3] Dr. Caldwell in his *Grammar of the Dravidian Languages*, p. 105.

Ctesias also refers to a lake in the country of the Pygmies upon the surface of which oil is produced. This is supposed to mean Upper Burma, where there is a tribe answering to this description, and where "there are also the only largely productive petroleum deposits, which, moreover, we know to have been worked since the earliest times."[1] Ctesias also mentions gold being obtained on certain "high-towering mountains" inhabited by the Griffins, which have been recognized as Tibetan mastiffs, "specimens of which, by the way, appear to have been taken to the Persian Court as examples of the gold-digging ants first described by Herodotus."[2]

---

[1] Professor Ball in the *I.A.*, vol. xiii., p. 230.

[2] *Ibid.*

CHAPTER II.

The Maurya Period.

We now reach the age of the Mauryas, which may be taken roughly to begin from the date of Alexander's Indian campaigns, about 325 B.C. In the accounts of these campaigns by Greek writers like Arrian, Curtius, and others, interesting light is sometimes thrown on the economic life of the period. Thus it may be stated with certainty that shipbuilding was in those very ancient days (so far back as 325 B.C.) a very flourishing industry giving employment to many, and the stimulus to its development must have come from the demands of both river and ocean traffic. Alexander's passage of the Indus was effected by means of boats[1] supplied by native craftsmen. A flotilla of boats was also used in bridging the difficult river of the Hydaspes.[2] For purposes of the famous voyage of Nearchus[3] down the rivers and to the Persian Gulf, all available country boats were impressed for the service, and a stupendous fleet was formed, num-

[1] V. A. Smith's *Early History of India*, p. 55.

[2] *Ibid.*, pp. 59, 60: "He found the fleet of galleys, boats, and rafts in readiness.' Also *Arrian*, v. 8.

[3] *Ibid.*, p. 87.

bering, according to Arrian,[1] about 800 vessels, according to Curtius and Diodorus about 1,000 vessels; but according to the "more reliable estimate of Ptolemy" nearly 2,000 vessels, which between them accommodated 8,000 troops, several thousand horses, and vast quantities of supplies. It was indeed an extraordinarily huge fleet, built entirely of Indian wood by the hands of Indian craftsmen. In this connection the remarks made by the two great authorities on the history of ancient Oriental commerce, namely Dr. Vincent and Dr. Robertson, are of considerable interest. Says Dr. Vincent :—

> The *Ayeen Akbari* reckons the Panje-ab as the third province of the Mogul Empire, and mentions 40,000 vessels employed in the commerce of the Indus. It was this commerce that furnished Alexander with the means of seizing, building, hiring, or purchasing the fleet with which he fell down the stream ; and when we reflect that his army consisted of 124,000 men, with the whole country at his command, and that a considerable portion of these had been left at the Hydaspes during the interval that the main body advanced to the Hyphasis and returned to the Hydaspes again, we shall have no reason to accuse Arrian of exaggeration when he asserts that the fleet consisted of 800 vessels of which 30 only were ships of war and the rest such as were usually employed in the navigation of the river. . . . Strabo mentions the proximity of Emodus, which afforded plenty of fir, pine, cedar, and other timber ; and Arrian informs us that Alexander in the country of the Assaconi, and before he reached the Indus, had already built vessels which he sent down the Koppenes to Taxila. All these circumstances contribute to prove the reality of a fact highly controverted ; and even though we were to extend the whole number of the fleet, comprehending tenders and boats, with some authors to 2,000, there is no improbability sufficient to excite astonishment.[2]

---

[1] *Indica*, ch. xix.

[2] *Commerce of the Ancients*, vol. i., p. 12.

Dr. Robertson also expresses the same opinion:—

> That a fleet so numerous should have been collected in so short a time is apt to appear at first sight incredible. But as the Punjab country is full of navigable rivers, on which all the intercourse among the natives was carried on, it abounded with vessels ready constructed to the conqueror's hands, so that he might easily collect that number. If we could give credit to the account of the invasion of India by Semiramis, no fewer than 4,000 vessels were assembled in the Indus to oppose her fleet (*Diod. Sicul.*, lib. ii., cap. 74). It is remarkable that when Mahmud of Ghazni invaded India, a fleet was collected on the Indus to oppose his, consisting of the same number of vessels. We learn from the *Ayeen Akbari* that the inhabitants of this part of India still continue to carry on all their communication with each other by water; the inhabitants of the Circar ot Tatta alone (in Sindh) have not less than 40,000 vessels of various construction.[1]

Further, we have the actual mention made by Arrian of the construction of dockyards, and the supply by the tribe called Xathroi of galleys of thirty oars and transport vessels which were all built by them.[2]

All this clearly indicates that in the age of the Mauryas shipbuilding in India was a regular and flourishing industry of which the output was quite large. The industry was, however, in the hands of the State and was a Government monopoly; for, as Megasthenes[3] informs us, while noticing the existence of a class of shipbuilders among the artisans, they were salaried public servants and were not permitted to work for any private person. These

---

1 *Disquisition concerning Ancient India*, p. 196.

2 *Anab.*, vi. 15, and *Curtius*, ix. 9.

3 *Strabo*, xv. 46: "But the armour-makers and shipbuilders receive wages and provisions from the kings for whom alone they work."

ships built in the royal ship-yards were, however, as Strabo[1] informs us, let out on hire both to those who undertook voyages and to professional merchants.

A few more interesting details regarding the shipping and navigation of the period are given by Pliny[2] in his description of Taprobane (Ceylon): "The sea between the island of Ceylon and India is full of shallows not more than six paces in depth, but in some channels so deep that no anchors can find the bottom. For this reason ships are built with prows at each end, for turning about in channels of extreme narrowness. In making sea voyages the Taprobane mariners make no observations of the stars, and indeed the Greater Bear is not visible to them, but they take birds out to sea with them which they let loose from time to time and follow the direction of their flight as they make for land."[3] Pliny also indicates the tonnage of these ancient Indian vessels, which is said to be 3,000 amphorae, the

---

[1] *Strabo*, xv. 46.

[2] *Pliny*, vi. 22, quoted in McCrindle's *Ancient India*, p. 55.

[3] *Pliny*, vi. 22. The fact of mariners using birds for ascertaining the direction in which the land lay is also alluded to in the *Digha Nikaya* (I. 222) of *Sutta-Pitaka*, the famous Pali text. Mr. Rhys Davids places the date of the *Digha* in the 5th century B.C. and takes this reference to be "the earliest in Indian books to ocean-going ships out of sight of land." (See *J.R.A.S.*, April, 1899, p. 432.)

amphora being regarded as weighing about a fortieth of a ton.[1]

The development of this national shipping made possible and necessary the creation and organization of a Board of Admiralty[2] as one of the six Boards which made up the War Office of Emperor Chandra Gupta (321 B.C. to 297 B.C.), "one of the greatest and most successful kings known to history." Fortunately, for information regarding this Board of Admiralty and the Naval Department we can depend not only on foreign notices like those of Megasthenes and Strabo, but also on the much more elaborate and reliable account given in the invaluable Sanskrit work of the period, the *Arthaśāstra* of Kautilya, which is undoubtedly one of the most important landmarks not only in the literary history of India but also in the history of Indian civilization itself. The book[3] requires to be thoroughly studied,

---

[1] *Pliny*, vi. 22. With regard to the equivalent of the amphora and the tonnage of these ancient vessels, McCrindle says: "The amount of cargo carried by ancient ships was generally computed by the talent or the amphora, each of which weighed about a fortieth of a ton. The largest ships carried 10,000 talents or 250 tons. The talent and the amphora each represented a cubic foot of water, and as the Greek or Roman foot measured about ·97 of an English foot, the talent and the amphora each weighed very nearly 57 lbs. See Torr's *Ancient Ships*, p. 25."

[2] V. A. Smith's *Early History of India*, p. 124. *Cf.* also *Strabo*, xv. 52: "Next to the city magistrates there is a third governing body which directs military affairs. This also consists of six divisions with five members to each. One division is associated with the Admiral of the Fleet."

[3] In using this book for my purposes I was greatly helped by the translations of Pandit R. Syāma Sāstry in the *Mysore Review*.

being a unique production of its kind in the entire Sanskrit literature, and a most valuable historical document, conveying as it does a perfectly complete picture of the extraordinarily rich and varied civilization that was developed in Maurya India over 2,000 years ago. I have, therefore, no hesitation in drawing largely upon the contents of this remarkable work of Chāṇakya and placing before the reader all such passages as tend to throw any light on the condition of the national shipping, navigation, and sea-borne trade of India in the glorious age of the Mauryas.

The Naval Department seems to have been very well organized. At its head was placed an officer who was called the नावध्यक्ष or the Superintendent of Ships.[1] He was entrusted with the duty of dealing with all matters relating to navigation, including not only *navigation of the oceans*, but also inland navigation on rivers and lakes, natural or artificial.[2] The matters relating to navigation were of course manifold. The Superintendent of Ships seems to have been something like a modern Port Commissioner, and his first duty was to see that all the dues of his port were paid, and not one evaded.

---

[1] *Arthaśāstra*, bk. ii., ch. xxviii.

[2] नावध्यक्षस्समुद्रसंयाननदीमुखतरप्रचारान्देवसरोविसरोनदीतरांश्च स्था-नीयादिष्ववेक्षेत ।

The kind and degree of the maritime activity of the period will be evident from the various kinds of port-taxes that were levied. Thus villages on sea-shores or on the banks of rivers and lakes had to pay regularly a fixed amount of tax.[1] Fishermen had to yield one-sixth of their haul as fees for fishing license.[2] Merchants also had to pay the customary tax levied in port towns.[3] Passengers arriving on board the State or the king's ship had to pay the fixed and requisite amount of sailing fees.[4] State boats were also let out to those who wanted to use them for pearl-fishery or for fishing for conch shells, and they had to pay the required amount of hire[5]; but they were also free to use their own boats for the purpose.[6] Besides these taxes payable to the Port Commissioner, there were the various sorts of ferry fees, which are also very interesting and equally indicative of a brisk trade and a throbbing commercial life. A man with a minor quadruped carrying some load had to pay a ferry

---

[1] तद्वेलाकूलग्रामाः क्लृप्तं दद्युः ।

[2] मत्स्यबन्धका नौकाहाटकं षड्भागं दद्युः ।

[3] पत्तनानुवृत्तं शुल्कभागं वणिजो दद्युः ।

[4] यात्रावेतनं राजनौभिः सम्पतन्तः ।

[5] शङ्खमुक्ताग्राहिणो नौकाहाटकान् दद्युः ।

[6] स्वनौभिर्वा तरेयुः ।

fee of one *masha*.[1] A load carried on the head, a load carried on the shoulders, a cow, and a horse had each to pay two *mashas*.[2] Four *mashas* were demanded for each camel or buffalo that was transported across the river.[3] Five *mashas* were levied for a small cart, six *mashas* for a cart of medium size that was drawn by bulls, and seven *mashas* for a big cart.[4] Four *mashas* had to be paid for a load of merchandise whether for sale or not.[5] Again, for big rivers involving greater risks, double the ferry fees above mentioned were charged.[6] Thus conveyances and beasts of burden as well as loads of merchandise were subject to ferry fees.

But besides seeing to the realization and collection of all proper taxes and dues, the Superintendent of Ships was also entrusted with the duty of enforcing many humane harbour regulations. Thus whenever any weather-beaten, tempest-tossed ship arrived at his port, his first duty was to lend her the protecting hand of a father.[7] He was also

---

[1] क्षुद्रपशुर्मनुष्यश्च सभारो माषकं दद्यात्।

[2] शिरोभारः कायभारो गवाश्वं च द्वौ।

[3] उष्ट्रमहिषं चतुरः।

[4] पञ्चलघुयानम्। षड्गोलिङ्गम्। सप्तशकटम्।

[5] पण्यभारः पादम्। तेन भाण्डभारो व्याख्यातः।

[6] द्विगुणो महानदीषु तरः।

[7] मूढवाताहतां तां पितेवानुगृह्णीयात्।

empowered to exempt from toll any ship laden with merchandise that was damaged and spoiled by water, or to charge only half the due toll, and then allow it to sail when the proper time for setting sail approached.[1] Again, whenever a ship laden with merchandise foundered owing to want of hands or on account of ill-repair, it was the duty of the Superintendent of Ships to make good the loss of merchandise in part or full, as the case might be, because presumably the loss was due not to any fault of the merchants but to defects in the State vessel, and therefore must be made good from State funds.[2]

But besides relieving ships in distress the Superintendent had to adopt many preventive measures to ensure safety. Thus during the period from the 7th day of Ashadha till the month of Kartika, i.e. when rivers are swollen owing to rains, the crossing of rivers by State or licensed ferries was strictly enforced.[3] Again, in those large rivers which cannot be forded during either the winter or summer seasons the Superintendent of Ships had to see that large and perfectly safe vessels were launched,

---

[1] उदकप्राप्तं पण्यमशुल्कमर्द्धशुल्कं वा कुर्य्यात् तथा निर्दिष्टाश्चैताः पण्यपत्तनयात्राकालेषु प्रेषयेत् ।

[2] पुरुषोपकरणहीनायामसंस्कृतायां वा नावि विपन्नायां नावध्यक्षो नष्टं विनष्टं वाभ्याभवेत् ।

[3] सप्ताहवृत्तमाषाढीं कार्त्तिकीं चान्तरा तरः ।
कार्म्मिकप्रत्ययं दद्यात् नित्यं चाह्निकमावहेत् ।

manned with all necessary officers and hands, viz. a captain, a steersman, and a number of servants who would hold the oars and the ropes and bale out water.[1] Small boats were launched only in small rivers that overflowed during the rainy seasons.[2]

To ensure safety there were also in force many strict regulations regarding the fording or crossing of rivers. Fording or crossing of rivers without permission was prohibited in order to ensure that no traitor or enemy could escape.[3] The time and even the place for fording and crossing rivers were definitely fixed, so that any person fording and crossing outside the proper place and in unusual times was punished with first amercement;[4] and the man who forded or crossed a river at the usual place and time but without permission had to pay a fine of 26¾ *panas*.[5] Exceptions to this stringent rule were, however, allowed in the interests of trade and public good. Thus the following[6] were

---

[1] शासकनिर्यामकदात्ररश्मिग्राहकोत्सेचकाधिष्ठिताश्च महानावो हेमन्तग्रीष्मतार्यासु महानदीषु प्रयोजयेत्।

[2] क्षुद्रिकासु वर्षास्राविणीषु क्षुद्रिकाः।

[3] बद्धतीर्थाश्चैताः कार्याः राजद्विष्टकारिणां तरणभयात्।

[4] अकालेऽतीर्थे च तरतः पूर्वः साहसदण्डः।

[5] काले तीर्थे च अनिसृष्टतारिणः पादोनसप्तविंशतिपणः तरात्ययः।

[6] कैवर्तकाष्ठतृणभारपुष्पफलवाटषण्डगोपालकानामनत्ययः सम्भाव्यदूतानुपातिनां च सेनाभाण्डप्रचारप्रयोगाणां च; स्वतरणैः तरतां; बीजभक्तद्रव्योपस्करांश्चानूपग्रामाणां तारयताम्।

freely allowed to cross rivers at any time and place:—

(1) Fishermen, whose business would be seriously hampered by the above regulations.

(2) Carriers of firewood, grass, flowers and fruits; gardeners and vegetable dealers who had to go far and wide to find the things they dealt in.

(3) Persons pursuing suspected criminals.

(4) Messengers following other messengers going in advance.

(5) Servants engaged to carry things (provisions and orders) to the army.

(6) Persons using their own ferries; and

(7) Dealers supplying villages of marshy districts with seeds, necessaries of life, commodities, and other accessory things. Again, Brahmans, ascetics, children, the aged and afflicted, royal messengers, and pregnant women had all to be provided by the Superintendent with free passes to cross rivers.[1] There was also another regulation permitting foreign merchants who had often been visiting the country, as also those who were well known to local merchants, to land freely in port towns.[2]

√ Lastly, the Superintendent of Ships was also entrusted with the duty of punishing all violations

---

[1] ब्राह्मणप्रव्रजितबालवृद्धव्याधितशासनहरगर्भिण्यो नावध्यक्ष मुद्राभिस्तरेयुः।

[2] कृतप्रवेशाः पारविषयिकाः सार्थप्रमाणा वा विशेयुः।

of harbour regulations, and miscreants that were dangerous to public peace. Thus to destruction were doomed the ships of pirates, the ships which were bound for the enemy's country, and the ships that violated the customs and rules in force in port towns.[1] The Superintendent had also to arrest persons of the following descriptions[2]: Any person who eloped with the wife or daughter of another; one who carried off the wealth of another; a suspected person; one having a perturbed appearance; one who had no baggage; one who attempted to conceal or evade the cognisance of a valuable load in his hand; one who had just put on a different garb; one who had just turned out an ascetic; one who pretended to be suffering from a disease; one who seemed to be alarmed; a person stealthily carrying valuable things; a person going on a secret mission; a person carrying weapons or explosives or holding poison in his hand; and lastly, one who came from a long distance without a pass. The Superintendent finally was to direct the confiscation of the commodities of those who were found to travel without a pass and of those also who with

---

[1] हिंस्रिका निर्घातयेत् । अमित्रविषयातिगाः पण्यपत्तनचारित्रोपघातिकाश्च ।

[2] परस्वभार्यां कन्यां वित्तं वापहरन्तं शङ्कितमाविग्नमुद्भाण्डीकृतं महाभाण्डेन मूर्ध्नि भारेणावच्छादयन्तं सद्योगृहीतलिङ्गिनमलिङ्गिनं वा प्रव्रजितमलक्ष्यव्याधितं भयविकारिणं गूढसारभाण्डशासनशस्त्राग्नियोगं विषहस्तं दीर्घपथिकममुद्रं चोपग्राहयेत् ।

a heavy load forded a river at an unusual place and time.[1]

We now have some idea of the organization of the Naval Department, the development of the national shipping, and the abounding commercial life in the India of the Mauryas. All this no doubt was due to the vast extent of the empire founded by Chandra Gupta that extended over the whole of Northern India from sea to sea, including even the provinces of the Paropanisadai, Aria, and Arachosia, beyond the modern frontiers of British India. The alliance of such a powerful emperor was courted even by the potentates of the Hellenistic world of his time. The consequence of this vast and varied realm was no doubt the constant stream of visitors, travellers, and envoys to and from India, and the resulting growth of elaborate regulations for their care and entertainment which were framed by the municipal commission under Chandra Gupta. "All foreigners were closely watched by officials, who provided suitable lodgings, escorts, and, in case of need, medical attendance."[2] As Mr. Vincent Smith remarks, "the existence of these elaborate regulations is *conclusive proof* that the Maurya Empire in the 3rd century B.C. was in

---

[1] निर्गच्छतामागच्छतश्च भाण्डं हरेयुः ।
अतिभारेणावेलायामतीर्थे तरतश्च ।

[2] V. A. Smith's *Early History of India*, p. 125.

constant intercourse with foreign states, and that large numbers of strangers visited the capital on business."[1] So great was the growth of foreign commerce that the mere taxes on imports formed a good and expanding source of revenue.

In the days of Asoka, whose empire embraced a much wider area than that of his grandfather, India was brought into systematic connection with the distant Hellenistic monarchies of Syria, Egypt, Cyrene, Macedonia, and Epirus,[2] and she soon became, through the efforts of merchants, and missionaries preaching the gospel of universal brotherhood, at once the commercial and spiritual centre, the very heart, of the Old World. This was possible only through the instrumentality of an efficient national shipping and system of communications. As Mr. V. A. Smith observes: "When we remember Asoka's relations with Ceylon and even more distant powers, we may credit him with a sea-going fleet as well as an army."[3]

In that monumental work called *Bodhisattvāvadāna Kalpalatā*, by the Kashmirian poet Kshemendra, of the 10th century A.D., is preserved a very interesting story regarding Indian mercantile activity in the Eastern waters, which clearly

---

[1] V. A. Smith's *Early History of India*, p. 125.

[2] *Rock Edicts* II. and XIII.

[3] *Edicts of Asoka*, Introduction, p. viii.

indicates that the progress of the foreign intercourse and naval activity of India during the days of the Emperor Chandra Gupta was continued also in the days of Asoka the Great. The 73rd Pallava or chapter of Kshemendra's work above referred to relates how the Emperor Asoka, seated on the throne in the city of Pataliputra, while holding his court, was one day approached by some Indian merchants who traded to the distant islands. They informed him of their losses and complete ruin brought about by the depredations of seafaring pirates called Nagas (probably the Chinese, who are worshippers of the Dragon), who destroyed all their ships and plundered their treasure. They said that if the Emperor was disposed to be indifferent to them they would no doubt be forced to take to other ways of earning their livelihood, but the imperial exchequer in that case was liable to be emptied owing to absence of sea voyages (i.e. if there was a slackening of the sea-borne trade and a consequent falling off in the export and import duties). Then the story goes on to relate how Asoka, after bestowing some thought on the seafaring Nagas, was persuaded by a Buddhist priest to issue a sort of edict (which we may call Asoka's *Marine Edict*) inscribed on a copper plate, which was, however, contemptuously set at naught by those for whom it was meant. It was only when Asoka became a devout Buddhist that he was able to make the Nagas respect his edict and give up all their booty, which was afterwards distributed among the merchants robbed.[1]

We have now narrated some of the facts in the sea-borne trade of India from the earliest times recorded to the glorious epoch of the Mauryas, seeking humbly to unroll the ample pages of one of the many forgotten but brilliant chapters in the early history of our country.

---

[1] राजा श्रीमानशोकोऽभूत्पुरे पाटलिपुत्रके ।

तं कदाचित् सभासीनं वणिजो द्वीपवासिनः ।
सर्वस्वनाशशोकार्त्ताः समेत्याशु व्यजिज्ञपुः ॥

अस्माकं तु प्रवहणं भंक्त्वा रत्नधनं हृतम् ।
केवलं नागद्वीपस्थैर्नागैः सागरवासिभिः ॥

वयमन्यत्र जीवामस्तदुपेक्षा तु ते विभो ।
समुद्रयात्राविच्छेदात् कोशक्षयविधायिनी ॥

इति तेषां वचः श्रुत्वा राजा संक्रान्ततद्व्यथः ।
समुद्रान्तर्गतान् नागान् विचिन्त्य स्तिमितोऽभवत् ॥

तं दृष्ट्वा निष्प्रतीकारकोपव्याकुलमानसम् ।
इन्द्रो नामाब्रवीद् भिक्षुः षडभिज्ञः स्थितोऽन्तिके ॥

नागानां रत्नचौराणां त्वत्प्रतापाभिरूपकः ।
तावत्पदार्पितो लेखः प्रेष्यतां पृथिवीपते ॥

इति भिक्षुवचः श्रुत्वा लेखं राजा विसृष्टवान् ।
क्षिप्तमेव तमम्बुधौ नागास्तीरे प्रचिक्षिपुः ॥

अथ राज्ञा पुनर्लेखे प्रहिते नागपुङ्गवाः ।
स्कन्धार्पिताखिलवणिग्धनभाराः समाययुः ॥

तदशेषं नरपतिर्वितीर्य्य वणिजां धनम् ।
विबुध्य नागानभवच्छिन्नग्रासमसादरः ॥

CHAPTER III.

The Andhra-Kushan Period: Intercourse with Rome.

The age of the Mauryas, of Chandra Gupta and Asoka, was followed by the age of the Andhras of the South and Kushans of the North, which witnessed an equal development of the foreign trade and intercourse of India. This is apparent not only from the writings of Greek, Roman, and other foreign authors, but also from the numismatic evidences discovered in India itself. With regard to the commerce of the Andhra period (200 B.C. to A.D. 250), R. Sewell, the well-known authority on the early history of Southern India, makes the following general remarks: "The Andhra period seems to have been one of considerable prosperity. There was trade, both overland and by sea, with Western Asia, Greece, Rome, and Egypt, as well as with China and the East. Embassies are said to have been sent from South India to Rome. Indian elephants were used for Syrian warfare. Pliny mentions the vast quantities of specie that found its way every year from Rome to India, and in this he is confirmed by the author of the *Periplus*. Roman coins have been found in profusion in the Peninsula, and especially in the south. In A.D. 68 a number of Jews, fleeing from Roman persecution, seems to have taken refuge among the friendly coast-people of South India, and to have settled in Malabar."[1] In respect of the same period, Dr. Bhandarkar, also, remarks, "trade and commerce must have been in a flourishing condition during this early period."[2]

In the north, under the Kushans, there was a great development of the intercourse of India with the West. "During the Kushana period the Roman influence on India was at its height. When the whole of the civilized world, excepting India and China, passed under the sway of the Caesars, and the Empire of Kaniska marched, or almost marched, with that of Hadrian, the ancient isolation of India was infringed upon, and Roman arts and ideas travelled with the stream of Roman gold which flowed into the treasuries of the Rajas in payment for the silks, gems, and spices of the Orient."[3]

The result of it was the rise of a new school of Indian art, the school of Gāndhāra, which is admitted on all hands to be closely related to the art of the Roman Empire in the Augustan and Antonine periods, and was at its best between A.D. 100–300. Indian coins were also affected like

---

[1] *Imperial Gazetteer*, New Edition, vol. ii., p. 325.

[2] *Early History of the Deccan*, p. 32.

[3] *J.R.A.S.*, January, 1903, p. 56.

Indian art. "Kadphises I., who struck coins in bronze or copper only, imitated, after his conquest of Kabul, the coinage either of Augustus in his later years, or the similar coinage of Tiberius (14 to 38 A.D.). When the Roman gold of the early emperors began to pour into India in payment for the silks, spices, gems, and dye-stuffs of the East, Kadphises II. perceived the advantage of a gold currency, and struck an abundant issue of Orientalized *aurei*, agreeing in weight with their prototypes, and not much inferior in purity. In Southern India, which during the same period maintained an active maritime trade with the Roman Empire, the local kings did not attempt to copy the imperial *aurei*, which were themselves imported in large quantities, and used for currency purposes just as English sovereigns are now in many parts of the world."[1]

Numismatic evidences point unmistakably to the growth of an active Indian commerce with the West, chiefly Rome. They also show that the main centre of this commercial activity was towards the south, in Tamilakam, the land of the Tamils, which figures so largely in the early history of the commerce of India. For we have already seen how, in the ancient days of Solomon, this land supplied the merchandise of his ships and kept up a commercial

---

[1] *Early History*, p. 238.

intercourse that has resulted in the incorporation of several Tamil words into the language of the Bible itself. The Roman coins found in Southern India in and near the Coimbatore district and at Madura are more numerous than the finds in the north.[1] The chief reasons for the dearth of coins in the north are that the export to Rome of which we have mention in classical writers, in exchange for which Roman coins were brought to India, was mostly of products of South India and the Deccan, while the Kushan kings had the Roman coins melted down in a mass and new coins issued from the metal having exactly the weight of the *aurei*. Besides this significance of these finds of Roman coins, one interesting feature[2] of the Andhra coins deserves to be carefully noted in this connection, conveying as it does a sure hint at maritime commerce, viz. that on many of these coins found on the east coast is to be detected the device of a two-masted ship, "evidently of large size," the suggestion of which is quite clear.

The stimulus to this Occidental trade of India came from the Roman Empire under Augustus.

---

1 "Roman Coins found in India," by Robert Sewell in the *J.R.A.S.*, 1904.

2 *Imperial Gazetteer*, New Edition, vol. ii., p. 324; V. A. Smith's *Early History*, p. 202: "Some pieces bearing the figure of a ship . . . suggest the inference that Yajna Sri's (184–213 A.D.) power was not confined to the land."

Before that time India carried on her trade chiefly with Egypt; whose king, Ptolemy Philadelphus (285–247 B.C.), with whom Asoka the Great had intercourse,[1] founded the city of Alexandria, that afterwards became the principal emporium of trade between East and West. With Alexandria communication was established of two seaports founded on the Egyptian coast, viz. Berenica and Myos Hormos, from which ships sailed to India along the coasts of Arabia and Persia. Strabo[2] mentions that in his day he saw about 120 ships sailing from Myos Hormos to India. There were of course other overland routes of commerce between India and the West, such as that across Central Asia along the Oxus to the Caspian and the Black Seas, or that through Persia to Asia Minor, or that by way of the Persian Gulf and the Euphrates through Damascus and Palmyra to the Levant. But this caravan traffic was by no means of any great importance, and was further reduced by the Parthian wars. "It was by the sea, and after Claudius by the open sea, that the bulk of merchandise from Indian south-coast ports was carried to the Arabian marts and Alexandria."[3] The Egyptian Greeks were the principal carriers of this extensive trade in Indian

---

[1] *Rock Edict* II.

[2] *Strabo*, ii. v. 12.

[3] "Roman Coins," *J.R.A.S.*, 1904.

commodities that sprang up under the Ptolemies, and as usual this commercial intercourse has left some marks on their language. Thus the Greek names for rice (*oryza*), ginger (*zingiber*), and cinnamon (*karpion*) have a close correspondence with their Tamil equivalents, viz. *arisi*, *inchiver*, and *karava* respectively; and this identity of Greek with Tamil words clearly indicates that it was Greek merchants who conveyed these articles and their names to Europe from the Tamil land. Again, the name *Yavana*, the name by which these Western merchants were known, which in old Sanskrit poetry is invariably used to denote the Greeks,[1] is derived from the Greek word *Iaones*, the name of the Greeks in their own language. The same word also occurs in ancient Tamil poems, and is exclusively applied to the Greeks and Romans. On this point the remarks of the late Mr. Pillay, our authority on Tamil literature, require to be quoted. He says: "The poet Nakkirar addresses the Pandyan prince Nan-Maran in the following words: 'O Mara, whose sword is ever victorious, spend thou thy days in peace and joy, drinking daily out of golden cups, presented by thy handmaids, the cool and fragrant wine brought by the Yavanas in their good ships.'" The *Yavanas* alluded to by these poets were undoubtedly the Egyptian Greeks, because, as stated

---

[1] Weber's *Indian Literature*, p. 220.

in the *Periplus*, it was Greek merchants from Egypt who brought wine, brass, lead, glass, etc., for sale to Muziris and Bakare, and who purchased from these ports pepper, betel, ivory, pearls, and fine muslins.[1] These Greek traders sailed from Egypt in the month of July and arrived at Muziris in forty days. They stayed on the Malabar coast for about three months and commenced their return voyage from Muziris in December or January.

The activity of this Occidental trade of India reached its height during the earlier days of the Roman Empire, especially the period from Augustus to Nero, the period of Rome's Asiatic conquests which made her a world power controlling the trade routes between the East and the West. Then a great demand arose on the part of the wealthy Romans for the luxuries of the East, which shocked the more sober-minded citizens of Rome. Thus we find Pliny[2] (about A.D. 77) lamenting and condemning the wasteful extravagance of the richer classes and their reckless expenditure on perfumes, unguents, and personal ornaments, saying that there was "no year in which India did not drain the Roman Empire of a hundred million sesterces,"[3] sending in return

---

[1] *The Tamils Eighteen Hundred Years Ago*, ch. iii.

[2] *Natural History*, xii. 18.

[3] £1,000,000, of which £600,000 went to Arabia and £400,000 to India; see Mommsen's *Provinces of the Roman Empire*, vol. ii., pp. 299–300.

wares which were sold for a hundred times their original value, "so dearly do we pay for our luxury and our women." What gave a great impetus to this Roman trade, and increased considerably its volume and variety, was, besides this steady and growing demand, the discovery of the regularity of the monsoons in the Indian Ocean. This discovery was made about the year 47 A.D. by a pilot named Hippalus,[1] and ships began to sail direct to the port of Muziris (Muyirikolu) in Malabar—a circumstance which added immensely to the security of the cargoes which no longer had to fear the attack of Arabs on caravans crossing the deserts or of pirates on vessels hugging the coast.

The articles of this Roman trade comprised chiefly (1) spices and perfumes, (2) precious stones and pearls, and (3) silks, muslins, and cotton. The consumption of aromatics in Rome was stimulated by religious and funeral customs. Incense was burnt at every worship. At the funeral of Sylla 210 loads of spices were strewn upon the pile. Nero is reported to have burnt at the funeral of Poppoea fully a year's produce of cinnamon and cassia. These spices were supplied to Rome by Arabians, who obtained them from India, famous from time immemorial as the land of aromatics. Pliny[2]

---

[1] *Periplus of the Erythraean Sea*, ch. lvii.

[2] *Natural History*, xii. 7 (14).

refers to the pepper[1] and ginger of India and the great demand for them in Rome, where they were bought by weight like gold and silver. Besides aromatics and spices, the articles for which there was a great inquiry in Roman markets were precious stones, pearls, and minerals, which have been carefully noticed and described by Pliny[2] with a skill rivalling that of a modern lapidary. The most highly prized of these stones was the beryl, found in India in only one place, namely Padiyur in the Coimbatore district, or at most in two, Vaniyambadi in the Salem district being said to also possess a mine; and these beryls were believed to be the best and purest in the world. And it is in the neighbourhood of these mines that the largest number of Roman coins has been found. Thirdly, the demand

---

[1] *Cf.* McCrindle, *Ancient India*, p. 121: "Pepper was in ancient times produced chiefly in those parts of India which adjoin the Malabar coast. The author of the *Periplus* names Tyndis, Muziris, Nelkynda, and Bacare as the ports from which pepper was exported. The ships, he tells us, which frequent these ports are of a large size on account of the great amount and bulkiness of the pepper and betel which form the main part of their cargoes." *Cf.* also Mommsen, *Provinces of the Roman Empire*, vol. ii., p. 301: "In the Flavian period, in which the monsoon voyages had already become regular, the whole west coast of India was opened up to the Roman merchants as far down as the coast of Malabar, the home of the highly esteemed and dear-priced pepper, for the sake of which they visited the ports of Muziris (probably Mangulura) and Nelcynda (in Indian doubtless *Nilkantha*, from one of the surnames of the god Shiva, probably the modern Nileswara). Somewhat farther to the south, at Kananor, numerous Roman gold coins of the Julio-Claudian epoch have been found, formerly exchanged against the spices destined for the Roman kitchens."

[2] *Natural History*, xxxvii. c. 1.

on India in Rome was also for silk, muslin, and cotton, which were sold at fabulously high prices. In the reign of Aurelian, silk was worth fully its weight in gold. Tiberius Caesar had to pass a law forbidding transparent silk as an indecent dress. Mr. Vincent A. Smith has thus summarized the information regarding the Roman trade with Southern India: "Tamil land had the good fortune to possess three precious commodities not procurable elsewhere, namely pepper, pearls, and beryls. Pepper fetched an enormous price in the markets of Europe. . . . The pearl-fishery of the Southern Sea, which still is productive and valuable, had been worked for untold ages, and always attracted a crowd of foreign merchants. The mines of Padiyur in the Coimbatore district were almost the only source known to the ancient world from which good beryls could be obtained, and few gems were more esteemed by both Indians and Romans. The Tamil states maintained powerful navies, and were visited freely by ships from both east and west, which brought merchants of various places eager to buy the pearls, pepper, beryls, and other choice commodities of India, and to pay for them with the gold, silver, and art ware of Europe."[1]

Numismatic evidences bring to light the fact that the Indian trade with Rome was most active

---

[1] *Early History*, p. 400.

during the period of eighty years from Augustus to Nero (A.D. 68); for the largest number of coins[1] discovered in Southern India refers to this period. As already noticed, the locale of these discoveries points also to the conclusion that the things which India exported comprised mostly spices and precious stones. In the long interval between Nero and Caracalla (A.D. 217) there must have been a decline of this trade, considering the very small number of coins discovered which belong to this period, and the finds have been mostly in cotton-growing districts, so that the conclusion is irresistible that the trade with Rome in such luxuries as spices, perfumes, and precious stones must have ceased after the death of Nero, and only a limited trade in necessaries, such as cotton fabrics, continued. This fact is almost in keeping with, and indeed explained by, the rise of a new era in social manners in Rome at this period under Vespasian, when, to use the words of Merivale, "the simpler habits of the Plebeians and the Provincials prevailed over the reckless luxury and dissipation in which the highest classes had so long

[1] According to Sewell, "Roman Coins," in the *J.R.A.S.* for 1904, "612 gold coins and 1187 silver, besides hoards discovered which are severally described as follows: of gold coins 'a quantity amounting to five cooly-loads'; and of silver coins (1) 'a great many in a plate,' (2) 'about 500 in an earthen pot,' (3) 'a find of 163,' (4) 'some,' (5) 'some thousands,' also (6) of metal not stated, 'a potfull.' These coins are the product of fifty-five separate discoveries, mostly in the Coimbatore and Madura districts."

indulged." The trade with Rome was at a low ebb from the days of Caracalla, when Rome was a prey to confusion, both internal and external, and her inhabitants could hardly think of spending large sums of money on spices, perfumes, and ornaments. There have been accordingly but few finds of coins belonging to this period, while the discoveries in the north are larger than in Southern or Western India. The Occidental trade revived again, though slightly, under the Byzantine emperors. The localities of the coins discovered suggest the conclusion that precious stones, cottons, and muslins were not in much request in Rome, but that an export trade was brisk in pepper and spices shipped from the southern ports both on the east and west. And so the fact need not surprise us that when Alaric spared Rome in A.D. 408 he demanded and obtained as part of the ransom 3,000 pounds of pepper.[1] The most interesting discoveries of this period are the finds at Madura, comprising two classes of Roman coins, the copper issues of the regular Roman coinage, and small copper coins locally minted for daily use; and the suggestion has been made that Roman commercial agents took up their residence in some of the capitals and marts of South India for trade purposes at a time when the Roman Empire was being overrun by barbarians. Vincent Smith is

---

[1] *Gibbon*, ch. xxxi.

also of the same opinion, and remarks[1]: "There is good reason to believe that considerable colonies of Roman subjects engaged in trade were settled in Southern India during the first two centuries of our era, and that European soldiers, described as powerful Yavanas, and dumb Mlecchas (barbarians) clad in complete armour, acted as bodyguards to Tamil kings, while the beautiful large ships of the Yavanas lay off Muziris (Cranganore) to receive the cargoes of pepper paid for by Roman gold." More interesting and conclusive is the evidence derived from the Tamil literature which may be adduced here in the words of Mr. Pillay again[2]: "Roman soldiers were enlisted in the service of the Pandyas and other Tamil kings." "During the reign of the Pandya Aryappadai-Kadantha-Nedunj-Cheliyan, Roman soldiers were employed to guard the gates of the fort of Madura."[3] A poet of this period describes a Tamil king's tent on a battlefield as follows: "A tent with double walls of canvas firmly held by iron chains, guarded by powerful Yavanas, whose stern looks strike terror into every beholder, and whose long and loose coats are fastened at the waist by means of belts, while dumb Mlecchas, clad in complete armour, who could express themselves only by

---

[1] *Early History of India*, pp. 400–401.

[2] *The Tamils Eighteen Hundred Years Ago*, ch. iii.

[3] *Chilappathikaram*, XIV. ii. 66–67.

gestures, kept close watch throughout the night in the outer chamber, constantly moving round the inner apartment, which was lighted by a handsome lamp."[1] It is evident from this description that Yavana and other Mlechchhas or foreigners were employed as bodyguards by ancient Tamil kings. Mr. Vincent Smith further says: "It is even stated, and no doubt truly, that a temple dedicated to Augustus existed at Muziris. Another foreign (Yavana) colony was settled at Kaviripaddanam, or Pukár, a busy port situated on the eastern coast at the mouth of the northern branch of the Kaviri (Cauveri) river. Both town and harbour disappeared long since, and now lie buried under vast mounds of sand. The poems tell of the importation of Yavana wines, lamps, and vases, and their testimony is confirmed by the discovery in the Nilgiri megalithic tombs of numerous bronze vessels similar to those known to have been produced in Europe during the early centuries of the Christian era, and by statements of the *Periplus*."

We have now dealt with the numismatic evidences that point unmistakably to the trade of India with Rome. But the fact of this Roman intercourse is further very satisfactorily established by the various references[2] we find in the native

---

[1] *Mullaipaddu*, ii. 59–66.

[2] These references have been dealt with in the *J.A.S.B.* for 1906, New Series, vol. ii., by Dr. Satischandra Vidyabhusana, M.A., Ph.D.

literature of India, in the ancient Sanskrit and Pali works, to Romaka or the city of Rome. Thus the *Mahābhārata* speaks of the Romaka or Romans coming to the Emperor Yudhisthira with precious presents on the occasion of the Rājasūya Yājña at Indraprastha or Delhi.[1] In the five famous astronomical works named *Paitāmaha*, *Vāśishtha*,[2] *Sūryya*,[3] *Paulisa*, and *Romaka Siddhāntas*, some of which were compiled in the 3rd or 2nd century A.D., Romaka is often mentioned as a *Mahāpuri*, *Pattana*, or *Visaya*, i.e. a great city, state, or dominion. Varāhamihira, who flourished about A.D. 505, also mentions Romaka in his well-known works *Pañcha-Siddhāntika* and *Vrihat-Sañhitā*. In a passage[4] in the former work he says that while there is sunrise at Lankā there is midnight at Romaka, and in the 16th chapter of the *Vrihat-Sañhitā* he speaks of the Romaka[5] or Romans standing under the influence of *chandra* or the moon. Lastly, in the Pali *Pitaka Romaka* is mentioned the *Romaka-Jātaka*, which describes a sham priest killing a pigeon to eat it

---

[1] औष्णीकाननुवासांश्च रोमकान् पुरुषादकान्
(*Mahābhārata*, *Sabha Parva*, ch. 51.)

[2] यमकोटिपुरीलङ्का रोमकाः सिद्धदाः क्रमात् ।

[3] पश्चिमे केतुमालाख्ये रोमकाख्या प्रकीर्त्तिता ।

[4] उदयो यो लङ्कायां · · रोमकविषयेऽर्द्धरात्रः सः ।

[5] गिरिसलिलदुर्गकोसलभरुकच्छसमुद्र रोमकतुषाराः ।

contrary to Buddhist practices, evidently to show the contrast of a Buddhist ascetic with a Roman ascetic.

Besides these evidences from ancient Indian works regarding the intercourse with Rome, there are also evidences from foreign works bearing on the subject. We have already referred to the enumeration and description of the vegetable and mineral products which India sent abroad, by Pliny, who calls India "the sole mother of precious stones," "the great producer of the most costly gems." Even as far back as 177 B.C., Agatharcides, who was President of the Alexandrian Library, and is mentioned with respect by Strabo, Pliny, and Diodorus, describes Sabaea (Yemen) as being the centre of commerce between Asia and Europe, and very wealthy because of the monopoly of the Indian trade. He also saw large ships coming from the Indus and Patala. But the more important works in this connection are undoubtedly the *Periplus of the Erythraean Sea* (A.D. 100) and Ptolemy's *Geography* (A.D. 140). The *Periplus*, a sort of marine guide-book, is the record of an experienced sailor who navigated the Red Sea, Persian Gulf, Malabar and Coromandel coasts, and resided for many years at Barygaza-Bharoach. According to the *Periplus*, Bharoach was the principal distributing centre of Western India, from which the merchandise brought from abroad was carried to the inland countries. Paithan, situated at twenty days' journey to the south of Barygaza, and Tagara, ten days' east of Pithan (modern Dharur in the Nizam's territory), were two inland towns of great commercial importance, of which the former sent into Bharoach for export waggons containing large quantities of onyx stones, and the latter ordinary cottons, muslins, mallow-coloured cottons, and other articles of local production. The other seaport towns mentioned in the *Periplus* are Souppara (modern Supara, near Bassein), Kalliena (modern Kalyan), a place by the way "of great commercial importance, since a good many of the donors whose names are inscribed in the caves at Kanhiri and some mentioned in the caves at Junnar were merchants residing in Kalyan,"[1] Semulla (identified with Chembur by some and Chaul by others), Mandagora (modern Mandad), Palaipatamai (probably Pal near Mahad), Melizeigara (modern Jayagad), and others. To the south three great emporia are mentioned, viz. Tyndis, Muziris, and Nelkynda, from which were exported pepper, spices, pearl, ivory, fine silks, and precious stones, such as diamonds, rubies, and amethysts. It may also be mentioned that the *Periplus* noticed large Hindu ships off East African, Arabian, and Persian ports

[1] *J.B.B.R.A.S.*, vol. vi.; *Arch. Sur. W. India*, No. 10; and Dr. Bhandarkar's *Early History of the Deccan*.

and Hindu settlements on the north coast of Sòcotra. In fact, as pointed out by Dr. Vincent, "in the age of the *Periplus*, the merchants of the country round Barygaza traded to Arabia for gums and incense, to the coast of Africa for gold, and to Malabar and Ceylon for pepper and cinnamon,[1] and thus completed the navigation of the entire Indian Ocean." The *Periplus* also throws some light on the shipping of the period. According to it, the inhabitants of the Coromandel coast traded in vessels of their own with those of Malabar, and at all seasons there was a number of native ships to be found in the harbour of Muziris. Three marts are mentioned on the Coromandel coast in which "are found the native vessels which make coasting voyages to Limurike—the monoxyla of the largest sort, called *sangara*, and others styled *colandiophonta*, which are vessels of great bulk and adapted to the voyages made to the Ganges and the Golden Chersonese."[2]

---

[1] *Commerce of the Ancients*, vol. ii., p. 404.

[2] Dr. Vincent makes the following interesting comment in this connection: "The different sorts of vessels constructed in these ports are correspondent to modern accounts; the monoxyla are still in use, not canoes, as they are improperly rendered; but with their foundation formed of a single timber, hollowed, and then raised with tiers of planking till they will contain 100 or 150 men. Vessels of this sort are employed in the intercourse between the two coasts; but the *colandiophonta*, built for the trade to Malacca, perhaps to China, were exceedingly large and stout, resembling probably those described by Marco Polo and Nicolo di Conti." Varthema likewise mentions vessels of this sort at Tarnasari (Masulipatam) that were of 1000 tons burthen (lib. vi., ch. 12) designed for this very

Some details are also given regarding the trade-routes. The ships carrying on the Indian trade started from Myos Hormos or Berenika, and sailed down the Red Sea to Mouza (twenty-five miles south of Mokha) and thence to the watering-place Okelis at the straits. They then followed the Arabian coast as far as Kane, passing on the way Eudaimon (Aden), Arabia, once a great mart for Indian traders. From Kane the routes to India diverge, some ships sailing to the Indus and on to Barygaza, and others direct to the ports of Limyrike (Malabar coast). There was also another route to Limyrike, starting from Aromata (Cape Guardafui). In all three voyages the ships made use of the monsoon, then called Hippalos, starting from Egypt in July.

Ptolemy's *Geography* describes the whole sea coast from the mouths of the Indus to those of the Ganges, and mentions many towns and ports of commercial importance. These are, among others, Syrastra (Surat), Monoglosson (Mangrol) in Guzerat, Ariake (Maharasthra),[1] Soupara, Muziris, Bakarei, Maisolia (Maslipatam), Kounagara (Konarak), and other places. Bishop Caldwell has pointed out that

---

trade to Malacca. The other vessels employed on the coast of Malabar, as Trapagga and Kotumba, it is not necessary to describe; they have still in the Eastern Ocean germs, trankees, dows, grabs, galivats, praams, junks. champans, etc." (*Commerce of the Ancients*, vol. ii., p. 521.)

[1] *Grammar of the Dravidian Languages*, p. 94.

in these three works, viz. Pliny's *Natural History*, the *Periplus*, and Ptolemy's *Geography*, is to be found the largest stock of primitive Dravidian words contained in any written documents of ancient times.

More interesting and reliable information regarding some of these South Indian ports is supplied by the Tamil literature of the times, in which are contained descriptions of their magnitude and magnificence which cannot fail to bring home to our minds the throbbing international life pervading entire Tamilakam. Thus Muchiri, an important seaport near the mouth of the Periyar, is described by a Tamil poet as follows: "The thriving town of Muchiri, where the beautiful large ships of the Yavanas, bringing gold, come splashing the white foam on the waters of the Periyar which belongs to the Cherala, and return laden with pepper."[1] "Fish is bartered for paddy, which is brought in baskets to the houses," says another poet: "sacks of pepper are brought from the houses to the market; the gold received from ships, in exchange for articles sold, is brought to shore in barges at Muchiri, where the music of the surging sea never ceases, and where Kudduvan (the Chera King) presents to visitors the rare products of the seas and mountains."[2] The description given of Kaviripaddinam (the Kamara

[1] *Erukkaddur Thayan Kannanar-Akam*, 148.

[2] *Oaranar-Puram*, 343.

of the *Periplus* and Khaberis of Ptolemy) or Pukar are equally important and inspiring. It was built on the northern bank of the Kaviri river, then a broad and deep stream into which heavily laden ships entered from the sea without slacking sail. The town was divided into two parts, one of which, Maruvar-Pakkam, adjoined the sea-coast. Near the beach in Maruvar-Pakkam were raised platforms and godowns and warehouses where the goods landed from ships were stored. Here the goods were stamped with the Tiger Stamp (the emblem of the Chola kings) after payment of customs duty, and passed on to merchants' warehouses.[1] Close by were the settlements of the Yavana merchants, where many attractive articles were always exposed for sale. Here were also the quarters of foreign traders who had come from beyond the seas and who spoke various tongues. Vendors of fragrant pastes and powders, of flowers and incense, tailors who worked on silk, wool, or cotton, traders in sandal, aghil, coral, pearl, gold, and precious stones, grain merchants, washermen, dealers in fish and salts, butchers, blacksmiths, braziers, carpenters, coppersmiths, painters, sculptors, goldsmiths, cobblers, and toy-makers—all had their habitation in Maruvar-Pakkam.[2] Another account thus describes the

---

[1] *Paddinappalai*, 134–136.

[2] *Chilappathikaram*.

markets of Kaviripaddinam: "Horses were brought from distant lands beyond the seas; pepper was brought in ships; gold and precious stones came from the northern mountains; sandal and aghil came from the mountains towards the west; pearls from the Southern seas, and coral from the Eastern seas. The produce of the regions watered by the Ganges; all that is grown on the banks of the Kaviri; articles of food from Elam or Ceylon and the manufacturers of Kalakam" (in Burma) were brought to the markets of Kaviripaddinam.[1] What is again worth noting is the fact that in these Chola ports there were lighthouses built of brick and mortar which exhibited blazing lights at night to guide ships to ports. It is also said that the palace of the Chola king in the city of Kaviripaddinam was built by "skilled artisans from Magadha, mechanics from Maradam, smiths from Avanti, carpenters from Yavana, and the cleverest workmen in the Tamil land."[2]

It may be noted in passing that in the period we are considering, India also maintained a sort of political connection with Rome, besides the commercial. Strabo[3] mentions that a mission or an embassy was sent to Augustus Caesar in 20 B.C. by

---

[1] *Paddinappalai*, 1–40.

[2] *The Tamils Eighteen Hundred Years Ago*, pp. 16, 24, 25, and 26.

[3] Book xv., ch. iv., 73.

the Indian king Pandion. It is now settled beyond doubt that Pandion was the king of the Pandyas of the south, who were then the only people in India that perceived the advantages of a European alliance that was first entered into in the days of the Mauryan emperors of Northern India. Strabo also mentions the name of Zarmano-Khegas, i.e. one of the Germanae, still called Sarmanes by the Hindus, as one of the ambassadors from Porus, king of 600 kings, to Augustus, who burnt himself at Athens; his epitaph was, "Here rests Khegas or Khegan the Jogue, an Indian from Barugaza (or Bhroach), who rendered himself immortal according to the custom of his country."[1] The embassies to Augustus are also alluded to by Dion Cassius,[2] by Florus,[3] and Orosius.[4] Dion Cassius[5] (A.D. 180) also speaks of Trajan receiving many embassies from Indians. With regard to this embassy Mr. Vincent A. Smith remarks: "The Indian embassy which offered its congratulations to Trajan after his arrival in Rome in 99 A.D. probably was dispatched by Kadphises II. to announce his conquest of North-Western India."[6]

---

[1] Dr. Vincent's *Commerce of the Ancients*, vol. i., p. 19.

[2] *Hist. Rome*, ix. 73.

[3] *Epitome of Roman History*, iv. 12.

[4] *History*, vi. 12.

[5] *Hist. Rome*, ix. 58. Dion Cassius also says (lxvii. 28): "Trajan having reached the ocean (at the mouth of the Tigris) saw a vessel setting sail for India."

[6] *Early History of India*, New Edition, p. 238.

Eusebius Pampheli[1] speaks of Indian ambassadors bringing presents to Constantine the Great; and Ammianus Marcellinus[2] of embassies sent by Indians to the Emperor Julian in 361 A.D.

The explanation of this intercourse of India with Rome is to be found in the fact that "from the time of Mark Antony to the time of Justinian, i.e. from B.C. 30 to A.D. 550, their political importance as allies against the Parthians and Ṣassanians, and their commercial importance as controllers of one of the main trade routes between the East and the West, made the friendship of the Kusans or Sakas, who held the Indus Valley and Baktria, a matter of the highest importance to Rome."[3] How close was the friendship is shown in A.D. 60 by the Roman general Corbulo escorting the Hyrcanian ambassadors up the Indus and through the territories of the Kushans or Indo-Scythians on their return from their embassy to Rome.[4] This close connection between India and the Roman Empire during the period of the Kushans also explains the mass of accurate information regarding the Indus valley and Bactria which Ptolemy in the 1st century A.D., and the author of the *Periplus* had been able to record, while it also accounts for the special value

---

[1] *De Vita Constant*, iv. 50.
[2] xxii. vii. 10.
[3] *Bombay Gazetteer*, vol. i., Part i., p. 490.
[4] Rawlinson's *Parthia*, 271.

of the gifts which the *Periplus* notices were set apart for the rulers of Sindh. One other result of this long-continued alliance was, as has been already indicated, the gaining by the Kushan and other rulers of the Peshawar and the Punjab of a knowledge of Roman coinage and astronomy.

After Pliny, Ptolemy, and the *Periplus*, the next important foreign notice of Indian commerce is that of Cosmas Indicopleustes (A.D. 535), which, though of a later date, may be most conveniently considered here. His *Christian Topography* furnishes some interesting particulars respecting Ceylon and the Malabar coast, included in which he preserves for us also a few Tamil words. He speaks of Mala or Malabar as the chief seat of the pepper trade, and mentions the five pepper marts of Poudopatana, Nalopatana, Salopatana, Mangarouth, and Parti, and also other ports farther northward on the western coast, such as Kallyan and Surat. He describes Ceylon under the name of Serendip as the place where "were imported the silk of Sinae-Roman China and the precious spices of the Eastern countries, and which were conveyed thence to all parts of India and to other countries." He then considers Ceylon [1] as the centre of commerce between China and the Gulf of Persia and the Red Sea. It was also "a great resort of ships from all

[1] McCrindle's *Ancient India*, p. 161.

parts of India and from Persia and Ethiopia, and in like manner it dispatches many of its own to foreign ports." He is the first Western author who "fully asserts the intercourse by sea between India and China,"[1] and alludes to the Eastern trade of India, of which we now must give an account.

---

[1] Dr. Vincent's *Commerce of the Ancients*, vol. ii., pp. 507–600.

CHAPTER IV.

The Period of Hindu Imperialism in Northern India under the Guptas and Harshavardhana—The Foundation of a Greater India: Intercourse with Farther India.

Throughout the centuries when India carried on her maritime and political intercourse with Rome she also maintained an equally active commerce with the farther East. The trade with the West alone was unable to give a full scope to her throbbing international life. We have already indicated some of the evidences supplied by Buddhist texts belonging to a period of a thousand years from 600 B.C., which all point to a complete navigation of the Bay of Bengal and the Indian Ocean and the flow of a steady and ceaseless traffic between Bengal and Ceylon, Madras and Burma. Those evidences have been set forth in great detail, and need not be reproduced here. As Elphinstone[1] has pointed out, "the inhabitants of the coast of Coromandel seem early to have been distinguished by

[1] *History of India*, p. 185.

their maritime enterprise from their countrymen on the west of India." Mr. Vincent Smith[1] also says: "Ancient Tamil literature and the Greek and Roman authors prove that in the first two centuries of the Christian era the ports on the Coromandal or Chola coast enjoyed the benefits of active commerce with both West and East. The Chola fleets did not confine themselves to coasting voyages, but boldly crossed the Bay of Bengal to the mouths of the Ganges and the Irrawaddy, and the Indian Ocean to the islands of the Malay Archipelago." Of the precise part played by the Tamils and their trade with Eastern nations, no detailed accounts are available, but according to our authority on this subject, Mr. Pillay, there are many allusions in ancient Tamil poems to voyages undertaken by merchants and others to Nagapuram in Chavakam (Sumatra or Java), Kalakam in Burma, and sea-ports in Ceylon and Bengal. Thus a ship sailing from the coast of Madura to Chavakam (Java) is said to have touched at Manipallavam, an island between Ceylon and India on which was one of the sacred seats of Buddha. Again, in another Tamil poem of the 1st century A.D. it is said that ships from Kalakan (the ancient name of Kaddaram in Burma) brought articles of merchandise to *Kaviripp-paddinam*, the great emporium at the mouth of the

---

[1] *Early History of India*, p. 415.

Kaveri.[1] Lower Burma or Pegu was conquered by emigrants from the Telugu kingdoms bordering on the Bay of Bengal, and consequently the people of Pegu have long been known to the Burmese and to all foreigners by the name of Talaing.[2]

Next to the Tamils in the eastward maritime activity of India the pioneering work seems to have been done and the lead taken by the ancient kingdom of Kalinga on the eastern sea-board, which is said to have been founded "at least eight centuries before Christ,"[3] and which extended from the mouth of the Ganges to the mouth of the Krishna. "It formed one of the five[4] outlying kingdoms of ancient India, with its capital about halfway down the coast and still surviving in the present city of Kalingapatam."[5] This kingdom was ruled for many centuries by princes of the Buddhist persuasion, a religion which did not tolerate any antipathy against foreign nations. The materials for the early history of this kingdom are mainly monumental in their character. Some of the inscriptions "speak of navigation and ship-commerce as forming part of the education of the princes of

---

[1] *Paddinappalai*, l. 191.

[2] Sir A. P. Phayre's *History of Burma*, pp. 28 and 31.

[3] Hunter's *Orissa*, p. 188.

[4] Viz. Anga, Banga, Kalinga, Shuma, and Pundra.

[5] Hunter's *Orissa*, vol. i., p. 170.

Kalinga."[1] The Chilka Lake in those days made an excellent harbour for anchorage, "crowded with ships from distant countries."[2] The conjecture may be hazarded that the great sea-king Bali of the *Rāmāyaṇa* might have been no other than a monarch of the sea-coast kingdom of Kalinga. At first confining their maritime efforts to Ceylon, the Klings from mere coasting soon began to make bolder voyages across the Bay of Bengal. From the evidences furnished by the *Buddhagat*, or the sacred scripture of the Burmese in particular, it is clear that a steady commercial intercourse was cultivated with Burma by the Buddhist merchants of Kalinga, which soon led to missionary undertakings for the propagation of their religion, and afterwards to the assumption of political supremacy in the land.[3] One of Asoka's religious missions was to Suvarna-bhumi or Burma, and one of the most famous of Hindu settlements, the remains of which still exist, was Thara-khetra

---

[1] Hunter's *Orissa*, vol. i., p. 197. Hunter remarks: "This and others of the inscriptions prove, in the opinion of the scholar to whom we owe their decipherings, that Kalinga was at that time an emporium of trade. We know from other sources that, shut out as Orissa was from the general policy of India, it boasted of fabrics which it could send as valuable presents to the most civilized monarchs of the interior. So fine was the linen which the prince of Kalinga sent to the King of Oudh, that a priestess who put on the gauzy fabric was accused of appearing naked." ("Cosma's Analysis of the Dulva," *Journal As. Soc. of Bengal*, vi., 1837.)

[2] *History of Puri*, by Brojokishore Ghosh.

[3] "History of the Burma Race," by Col. Sir A. Phayre, *A.S.J.*, no. 1, 1864, and no. 2, 1868.

near Prome.[1] According to R. F. St. Andrew St. John,[2] "somewhere about 300 A.D. people from the west coast of the Bay of Bengal founded colonies on the coasts of the Gulf of Martaban, of which the principal appears to have been Thaton or Saddhammanagara." The intercourse between Kalinga and Burma also appears from Sir A. P. Phayre's statement of coins and medals with Hindu symbols being found in Pegu.[3] "That there was intercourse also with Malacca is evident from many words in the Malayan language which Marsden has traced to an Indian or Sanskrit origin. To this day there are Klings or descendants of settlers from ancient Kalinga at Singapore." The Klings are the lowest class of Indians, and their name is derived from Kalinga in India, from whence they are said to have come. Indians, moreover, of a higher grade, Madrasees, Tamils, etc., are also called Klings at Singapore.[4] With reference to this ancient trade Sir Walter Elliot observes: "There is no doubt that the intercourse between the east coast of India and the whole of the opposite coast of the Bay of Bengal and the Straits of Malacca was far greater in ancient times. . . . It had attained its height at the time the Buddhists were in the ascendant, i.e. during

---

1 "History of the Burma Race," by Col. Sir A. Phayre in *A.S.J.*

2 *J.R.A.S.*, 1898.

3 *History of Burma*, p. 31.

4 *Mission Life*, May, 1867.

the first five or six centuries of our era. The first great Buddhist persecution both checked it and also drove great numbers of the victims to the opposite coast. The Tamil and Telugu local histories and tradition are full of such narratives. When the Chalukya prince, brother of the King of Kalyan, was founding a new kingdom at Rajamundry, which involved the rooting out and dispersion of the pre-existing rulers, nothing is more probable than that some of the fugitives should have found their way to Pegu. One Tamil MS. refers to a party of Buddhist exiles, headed by a king of Manda, flying in their ship from the coast."[1]

---

[1] Sir A. P. Phayre, "History of Pegu," in *A.S.J.*, 1873.

CHAPTER V.

The Period of Hindu Imperialism in Northern India (*continued*): The Colonization of Java.

Perhaps the most interesting and conspicuous fact in connection with the Indian maritime activity towards the East is the Hindu colonization of Java, one of the most glorious achievements recorded in the entire history of the country. And yet the first impulse to this colonizing activity and expansion of India had its origin in the obscure kingdom of Kalinga, whose early history nobody knows or cares to know. As far back as the 75th year of the Christian era a band of Hindu navigators sailed from Kalinga, and, instead of plying within the usual limits of the Bay of Bengal, boldly ventured out into the open limitless expanse of the Indian Ocean and arrived at the island of Java. There the adventurous navigators planted a colony, built towns and cities, and developed a trade with the mother country which existed for several centuries. The history of this Hindu colonization of Java is thus briefly put by Elphinstone: "The histories of Java give a distinct account of a numerous body of Hindus from Clinga (Kalinga) who landed on this island, civilized the inhabitants, and who fixed the date of their arrival by establishing the era still subsisting, the first year of which fell in the 75th year after Christ. The truth of this narrative is proved beyond doubt by the numerous and magnificent Hindu remains that are still existing in Java, and by the fact that, although the common language is Malay, the sacred language, that of historical and political compositions and of most inscriptions, is a dialect of Sanskrit. The early date is almost as decisively proved by the journal of the Chinese pilgrim in the end of the 4th century who found Java entirely peopled by Hindus, and who sailed from the Ganges to Ceylon, from Ceylon to Java, and from Java to China in ships manned by crews professing the Brahminical religion."[1]

That Kalinga had a large share in the colonization of Java and the adjacent islands is hinted at not only in the native chronicles of Java but is also accepted as truth by many competent scholars. Crawford (A.D. 1820) held that all Hindu influence in Java came from Kalinga or North-East Madras. Fergusson[2] also observes: "The splendid remains at Amravati show that from the mouths of the Krishna and Godavari the Buddhists of North and North-West India colonized Pegu, Cambodia,

---

[1] *History of India*, Cowell's Edition, p. 185.

[2] *Indian Architecture*, p. 103.

and eventually the island of Java." Tavernier[1] in A.D. 1666 remarked that "Masulipatam is the only place in the Bay of Bengal from which vessels sailed eastwards for Bengal, Arrakan, Pegu, Siam, Sumatra, Cochin China, and the Manillas, and west to Hormuz, Makha, and Madagascar." Inscriptions also bear out the correctness of the connection between the Kalinga coast and Java which Java legends have preserved.[2] Besides, as Dr. Bhandarkar has pointed out[3] in his article on the eastern passage of the Sakas, certain inscriptions also show a Māgadhi element which may have reached Java from Sumatra, and Sumatra from the coast either of Bengal or Orissa. It is further observed, in the *Bombay Gazetteer*, that "the Hindu settlement of Sumatra was almost entirely from the east coast of India, and that Bengal, Orissa, and Masulipatam had a large share in colonizing both Java and Cambodia cannot be doubted."[4]

There is, however, another legend preserved in the native chronicles of Java which transfers the credit of its colonization from Kalinga on the eastern coast to Gujarat on the west. According

---

[1] Ball's Translation, 1, 174

[2] *Indian Antiquary*, v. 314, vi. 356; referred to in the *Bombay Gazetteer*, vol. i., Part i., p. 496.

[3] *Journal*, Bombay Branch of R.A.S., xvii.

[4] Vol. i., Part i., p. 493.

to this legend, a great and powerful prince from Gujarat named Aji Saka made his descent on the island about A.D. 75, but was soon compelled to withdraw in consequence of a pestilence or some other calamity. This story was perhaps invented only to show the connection of the ancient royal dynasty of Java with the Saka kings of Northern India. The Javanese chronicles, however, record, besides this abortive attempt, another more successful attempt[1] at colonization, made again from the west coast of India, about A.D. 603, when a ruler from Gujarat, forewarned of the coming destruction of his kingdom, started his son with five thousand followers, among whom were cultivators, artisans, warriors, physicians, and writers, in six large and a hundred small vessels towards Java. After some difficulty they got to the western coast of Java, and built there the town of Mendang Kumulan. The son soon sent for more men to his father, who dispatched a reinforcement of 2,000, including carvers in stone and brass. An extensive commerce sprang up with Gujarat and other countries, and the foundations were laid of temples that were afterwards known as Prambanam and Borobudur, the grandest specimens of Buddhist art in the whole of Asia. These legendary facts are probably connected with some central event in a process which continued

[1] *History of Java*, by Sir Stamford Raffles, vol. ii., p. 82.

for at least half a century before and after the beginning of the 7th century, a process of Saka migration that was stimulated by the then condition of Northern India, and was almost a sequence of the final collapse of the Saka power at the beginning of the 5th century, when the Saka kingdom of Surashthra or Kathiawar was conquered by Chandra Gupta II.,[1] and Brahmanism supplanted Buddhism as the dominant State religion in India. Then "the Buddhist art-traditions went with the Saka immigrants into Java, where they reached their highest expression in the magnificent sculpture of Borobudur."[2] There were, however, other forces at work which conspired to bring about a general movement among Northern Indians. The defeat of the White Hunas by Sassanians and Turks between A.D. 550 and 600 intercepted their retreat northwards; secondly, there were the conquests of Prabhākaravardhana, the father of S'rī-Harsha of Magadha, who defeated the king of Gāndhāra, the Hunas, the king of Sindh, the Gurjjaras, the Latas, and the king of Malava; and thirdly, there followed close upon them the further defeats inflicted by S'rī-Harsha himself about twenty years later (A.D. 610–642), so that there would be quite swarms of refugees at the Gujarat ports eager to escape further

[1] See V. A. Smith's *Early History of India*, pp. 186, 187.

[2] *Indian Sculpture and Painting*, by E. B. Havell, p. 113.

attack and to share in the prosperity of Java. If we add to these the following further events which all took place during the second half of the 7th century, viz. the advance of the Turks from the north, and of the Arabs both by sea (A.D. 637) and through Persia[1] (A.D. 650–660), the conquering progress[2] of a Chinese army from Magadha to Bamian in A.D. 645–650, the overthrow (A.D. 642) of the Buddhist Saharais by their usurping Brahmanist minister Chach, and his persecution of the Jats, we have a concatenation of circumstances which sufficiently explains the resulting movement, fairly constant, of Northern Indians southwards from the ports of Sindh and Gujarat, a movement which, though caused by fear, would be strengthened by the tidings of Javan prosperity reaching the leaders. For the same enterprise and ambition that led Alexander to put to sea from the mouths of the Indus, Trajan from the mouth of the Tigris, and Mahmud of Ghazni from Somnath, must also have driven the

---

[1] In 637 A.D. raiders attacked Thana from Oman and Bhroach, and Sindh from Bahrein.—Reinaud's *Mémoire sur l'Inde*, 170, 176.

[2] The Chinese emperor sent an ambassador, Ouang-h-wuentse, to Śrī-Harsha, who, on his arrival, found he was dead (A.D. 642) and his place usurped by a minister who drove him off. The envoy retired to Tibet, and with help from Tibet and Nepal he returned, defeated the usurper, and pursued him to the Gandhara river. The passage was forced, the army captured, the king, queen, and their sons were led prisoners to China, and 580 cities surrendered; the magistrates proclaimed the victory in the Temple of the Ancients, and the emperor raised the rank of the triumphant ambassador.

Saka, Huna, and Gurjjara chiefs to lead their men south to the land of rubies and gold.[1]

---

[1] In comparing the relative importance of the western and eastern Indian strains in Java, it is to be remembered that the western element has been overlaid by a late Bengal and Kalinga layer of fugitives from the Tibetan conquest of Bengal in the 8th century and during the 9th and later centuries by bands of Buddhists withdrawing from a land where their religion was no longer honoured.—*Bombay Gazetteer*, vol. i., p. 498.

HINDU PERIOD

CHAPTER VI.

THE PERIOD OF HINDU IMPERIALISM IN NORTHERN INDIA (*continued*): THE MARITIME ACTIVITY OF THE BENGALIS.

THERE was also another people that played a very prominent part in the sea-borne trade and colonizing activity of India towards the East. The testimony that history bears to the military, religious, and maritime enterprise and achievements of the ancient Buddhistic Bengali in the earlier centuries of the Christian era now scarcely wins belief and acceptance. Yet it is an incontrovertible fact that Bengal of old gave birth to men who marched armies beyond the frontiers of modern India and ruled for a time as the paramount power in the land; who braved the perils of the deep in armed galleys, and carried home foreign itinerants in their ships. It is also equally noteworthy that from very early times she has been the home of many a religious movement whose influence penetrated to lands far beyond her limits. It is hardly sufficiently known that during the first few centuries of the Christian era an enthusiastic band of devoted Bengalis, burning with a proselytizing zeal, went as far as China, Corea, and Japan, carrying with them the torch of the

Buddhistic faith, while her Buddhistic scholars and reformers, like Atīsha, Dīpaṅkara, and S'īlabhadra, achieved an Asiatic fame, and were known throughout the wider Buddhistic world. It is also a recent discovery that some of the scriptures of the Japanese priests preserved in the Horiuzi temple of Japan are written in Bengali characters of the 11th century,[1] thus testifying to the extraordinary vitality of Bengali religious activity that made itself felt even in the Land of the Rising Sun. Artists and art-critics also see in the magnificent sculptures of the Burobudur temple in Java the hand of Bengali artists who worked side by side with the people of Kalinga and Gujarat in thus building up its early civilization. And the numerous representations of ships which we find in the vast panorama of the bas-reliefs of that colossal temple reveal the type of ships which the people of Lower Bengal built and used in sailing to Ceylon, Java, Sumatra, China, and Japan, in pursuit of their colonizing ambition, commercial interests, and artistic and religious missions. The *Mahāwaṅsa* and other Buddhistic works tell us how as early as about 550 B.C. Prince

---

[1] The priests of the temple worship the manuscript of a Buddhistic work called *Usñisa Vijaya Dharmi*, written in a character considered by experts to be identical with that prevalent in Bengal in the 6th century. Vide *Anecdota Oxoniensis*, vol. iii. For information regarding this and some other points connected with ancient Bengali enterprise, I am indebted to Srijukta Dineshchander Sen, the learned author of the *History of Bengali Literature*.

Vijaya of Bengal with his 700 followers achieved the conquest and colonization of Ceylon, and gave to the island the name of Siṅhala after that of his dynasty—an event which is the starting-point of Sinhalese history. It is also said that in a still earlier period the Bengalis of Chāmpā, near Bhagalpur, founded a settlement in Cochin China, and named it after their famous native town.[1] No less creditable also were the artistic achievements of Bengal;[2] besides, as we have seen, influencing the art of Borobudur, Bengali art has influenced that of Nepal through the schools of painting, sculpture, and works in cast metal founded about the middle of the 9th century by Dhīman and his son Bitpāl, inhabitants of Barendra, and from Nepal the art of the Bengali masters spread to China and other parts of the Buddhistic world.

This tradition of Bengalis being once famous for their maritime enterprises and commercial activities has also been, as may be naturally expected, well preserved in their literature. No folk-lore is so popular in Bengal as those volumes of poetry evoked by devotion to the goddesses of

---

[1] Rhys David's *Buddhist India*, p. 35.

[2] *Indian Antiquary*, vol. iv., p. 101. Mr. Havell, in his *Indian Sculpture and Painting*, writes: "From the seaports of her eastern and western coasts India sent streams of colonists, missionaries, and craftsmen all over Southern Asia, Ceylon, Siam, and far-distant Cambodia. Through China and Korea Indian art entered Japan about the middle of the 6th century."

Chaṇḍī and Manasā, and in them are contained accounts of the maritime adventures of merchants like Dhanapati, S'rīmanta, and Chand Saodāgara, which, in spite of the miraculous details invented and imported into them by a pious imagination and warm religious feeling, contain a nucleus of truth, and unmistakably point to one of the ways through which the national genius of the country chose to express itself. In the same manner that Shakespeare's Antonio had "an argosy bound for Tripoly, another for the Indies, a third for Mexico, and a fourth for England," is our Indian S'rīmanta represented to possess merchantmen trading to the Coromandel coast, to Ceylon, to Malacca, Java, and China. The vast collection of poems known as the *Padma Purāṇa* or *Manasāmaṅgala* is formed by the contributions of more than fifty authors who have all described sea voyages. About eight or nine poems form the group of poems celebrating the glories of the goddess Chaṇḍī, and in nearly all of them are also contained accounts of sea voyages. These works belong to so late a period as the 16th century, and their value lies in the fact that they thus carry down to comparatively late times the tradition of the Bengalis being once known for their commercial and maritime pursuits. The oldest record in Bengali literature is that of Nārāyaṇadeva, a poet who lived about the latter part of the 13th century, and who has given a graphic account of the sea voyage of Chand Saodāgara. Another account, free from exaggerations and fabulous details, and hence more reliable, is that given by Baṅśī Dasa, who of course profusely borrows from Nārāyaṇadeva.

These poems together throw a great light on the then condition of commerce in Bengal. Sailors for sea-going vessels were then, as now, recruited from the people of East Bengal, who have been the object of genial banter in the writings of Kavikaṅkana, Ketakadāsā, Kshemānanda, and others. Ships had more poetical names in those days than now. In *Manasāmaṅgala* poems we come across such names as *Gaṅgāprasād* (গঙ্গাপ্রসাদ), *Sāgarafenā* (সাগরফেনা), *Haṅsarava* (হংসরব), *Rājavallava* (রাজবল্লভ), and the like. There is a very detailed account of the fleet of Dhanapati sailing towards Ceylon in *Kavikaṅkaṇa Chaṇḍī*, which is well worth a notice.[1] It

---

[1] প্রথম তুলিল ডিঙ্গা নাম মধুকর
শুধাই স্নুবর্ণে তার বসিবার ঘর।
আর ডিঙ্গা তুলিলেক নাম দুর্গাবর।
তবে তোলে ডিঙ্গাখানি নাম গুয়ারেখি।
দ্বিপ্রহরের পথে যার মাথা কাঠ দেখি॥
আর ডিঙ্গা তুলিলেক নাম শঙ্খচূড়।
আশি গজ পানি ভাঙ্গি গাঙ্গে লয় কূল।
তবে ডিঙ্গাখান তোলে নাম সিংহমুখী।
সূর্য্যের সমানরূপ করে ঝিকিমিকি॥
আর ডিঙ্গা তুলিলেক নাম চন্দ্রপান।
তাথে ভরা দিলে দুই কূলে হয় থান॥

is made up of seven vessels. The head ship is called *Madhukara* (মধুকর), generally meant for princes and big merchants: its cabin is made all of gold. The second ship is named *Durgāvara*, the third *Gooarākhi*, the fourth *Saṅkshachūra*, the fifth *Siṅhamukhī*, shining like the sun, the sixth *Chandrapāna*, which is used for goods, and the seventh *Chotamukhī*, meant to carry provisions.[1] The whole fleet sailed merrily, propelled by the lustily singing oarsmen. There were also trading fleets carrying merchandise and provisions for long voyages; and worthless things were often exchanged in distant countries for very valuable ones.[2]

The great trading centres of Bengal in those

আর ডিঙ্গা তুলিলেক নামে ছোটমুখী।
তাহে চালু ভরা চাহে হাজার এক পুটী।
সম ধুনা দিয়া তবে গাইল সাত নায়।
তড়িৎ গমনে ডিঙ্গা সাজিয়া চালায়॥
সাতখানি ডিঙ্গা ভাসে ভ্রমরার জলে।
গোঁজে বাঁধি রাখে ডিঙ্গা লোহার শিকলে॥
তার পিছে চলে ডিঙ্গা নাম চন্দ্রপাট।
যাহার উপরে চাঁদ মিলায়েছে হাট॥ (বিজয় গুপ্ত)

[1] মুলার বদলে দিল গজদন্ত। (বিজয় গুপ্ত)

[2] শুক্তার বদলে মুক্তা দিল
ভেড়ার বদলে ঘোড়া॥ (কবিকঙ্কণ)

days were Satgaon, called *Tcharitrapoura* in the time of the Chinese pilgrim's visit, and described by Ptolemy as a royal city of immense size, as well as *Sonargaon*, the great harbour of Eastern Bengal. Chāmpa or Bhagalpur was also one of the commercial centres from which merchants could sail for *Subarṇabhūmi* or the Burmese coast. But by far the most important emporium of ancient Bengal was Tamralipta, the great Buddhist harbour of the Bengal sea-board. It is referred to in the *Mahāwaṅso* (ch. xix.) as Tamalitta, and was probably meant by the author of *Periplus* when he spoke of "a great commercial city near the mouth of the Ganges, the trade of which consisted chiefly in cloths of the most delicate texture and extreme beauty." The place is of very great antiquity, and existed prior to the days of Asoka, for it figures even in the sacred writings of the Hindus. The Chinese pilgrim, Fa-Hien, when he visited India in A.D. 399–414, found it a maritime settlement of the Buddhists. "There are twenty-four Sangharamas in this country," he says; "all of them have resident priests." After his residence there for two years he shipped himself on board a great merchant vessel which he found in the harbour of Tamluk, and putting to sea, they proceeded in a south-westerly direction, and catching the first fair wind of the winter season (i.e. of the N.E. monsoon), they sailed for fourteen days and nights, and arrived at Ceylon. Two hundred and fifty years later, a yet more celebrated pilgrim from China speaks of Tamluk as still an important Buddhist harbour, with ten Buddhist monasteries, a thousand monks, and a pillar by Asoka 200 feet high. It was "situated on a bay, could be approached both by land and water, and contained stores of rare and precious merchandise and a wealthy population." And another Chinese traveller, I-Tsing, who followed Hiuen Tsang, thus wrote of the Bengal port: "Tamalipti is forty *yojanas* south from the eastern limit of India. There are five or six monasteries; the people are rich. . . . This is the place where we embarked when returning to China."[1]

[1] Takakusu's *I-Tsing*, xxxiii., xxxiv.

CHAPTER VII.

THE PERIOD OF HINDU IMPERIALISM IN NORTHERN INDIA (*continued*): THE INTERCOURSE WITH CHINA.

IT was also in the age of the Guptas and Harshavardhana that we find the field of Indian maritime activity in the eastern seas extending as far as China and Japan in the farthest East, beyond the small colonies of Java and Sumatra. As Mr. Kakasu Okakura remarks, "Down to the days of the Mohammedan conquest went, by the ancient highways of the sea, the intrepid mariners of the Bengal coast, founding their colonies in Ceylon, Java, and Sumatra, and binding Cathay (China) and India fast in mutual intercourse."[1] The intercourse of India with China by way of the sea began at least as early as the commencement of the Christian era, while "the Chinese did not arrive in the Malay Archipelago before the 5th century, and they did not extend their voyages to India, Persia, and Arabia till a century later."[2] Throughout the

[1] *Ideals of the East*, pp. 1, 2.

[2] Mr. G. Phillips in the *J.R.A.S.*, 1895, p. 525. According to Professor Lacouperie (*Western Origin of Chinese Civilization*) the maritime intercourse of India with China dates from a much earlier period, from about 680 B.C., when the "sea-traders of the Indian Ocean," whose "chiefs

1st and 2nd centuries of the Christian era, during the reigns of the Chinese Emperor Hoti (A.D. 89–105) and of the Emperor Hiwanti (A.D. 158–9), there arrived, according to Chinese annals, many embassies from Indian sovereigns bringing merchandise under the name of tribute to the Chinese court, which alone had the monopoly of the trade with foreign nations.[1] Thus, as the *Milinda Panha* informs us (pp. 127, 327, 359), during the 2nd century after Christ, when under the great Satrap Rudradaman (A.D. 143–158) the Kshatrapa dynasty of Kathiavad was at the height of its power, challenging the supremacy even of the great Andhra Empire, Indians of the Tientes, i.e. Sindhu, brought presents by sea to China. Chinese annals point also to a continued intercourse of Ceylon with China by way of the sea, which was due to a common national worship. Among those men who shared in the propagation of Buddhism and in the

---

were Hindus," founded a colony called *Lang-ga*, after the Indian name *Lanka* of Ceylon, about the present Gulf of Kiao-tchoa, where they arrived in vessels having the prows shaped like the heads of birds or animals after the patterns specified in the *Yuktikalpataru* and exemplified in the ships and boats of old Indian art. These Indian colonists had, however, to retreat before the gradual advance of the Chinese till they became merged in the kingdom of Cambodia, founded by Hindus in the Indo-Chinese peninsula about the 1st century A.D. But throughout this period the monopoly of the sea-borne trade of China was in their hands, and the articles of this trade were the well-known Indian products, such as rubies, pearls, sugar, aromatics, peacocks, corals, and the like.

[1] See *J.R.A.S.*, 1896, pp. 64–66.

translations of its scriptures in China, there were many who took the sea route between India and China. Some particulars about them are contained in the *Kwai-Yuen Catalogue* of the Chinese Tripitaka compiled in A.D. 730.[1] The first eminent Buddhist who succeeded in finishing a sea journey from Ceylon to China was of course the well-known Fa-Hien. But a little before him an Indian called Buddhabhadra, a descendant of the Sakya prince Amitodana, arrived in China in 398, i.e. two years before Fa-Hien entered India. He embarked from Cochin for China after travelling through Northern India and Indo-China. After him the *Kwai-Yuen Catalogue*, as well as other Chinese works, mentions a series of names of Buddhist priests who sailed between Southern India and China. Thus in A.D. 420 Saṅghavarmi, a Sinhalese and the translator of the *Mahisasaka Vinaya*, arrived in China. In A.D. 424 Gunavarman, grandson of an ex-king of Kabul, arrived at the capital of the Sung dynasty. He had sailed from Ceylon and visited Java on the way, like Fa-Hien. In the year 429 A.D., in the reign of the Emperor Wun, three Sinhalese visited China. Again, it is mentioned in the work called *Bhikshuni Nidāna* that in the year 433 A.D. the ship called *Nandi* brought to China a second party of Sinhalese nuns who established the Bhikshuni

---

[1] Professor M. Anesaki in the *J.R.A.S.*, April, 1903.

order in China. In A.D. 434 there arrived in China quite a number of Sinhalese nuns, under the leadership of a certain Tissara, to further Gunavarman's work for the foundation of the monastic system in China after the model of Sinhalese Buddhism. In A.D. 435 Gunabhadra, the translator of the *Saṅyukta-āgama* (of which the MS. was brought by Fa-Hien from Ceylon), arrived at the province of Kau in China from Ceylon. Again, in A.D. 438 another group of eight Bhikshunis came from Ceylon. In A.D. 442 Saṅghavarman, who had come to China by the overland route, sailed from the southern coast of China for India. In A.D. 453 a Chinese Buddhist called Dharmakrama took the sea route from Southern India on his way back to China. Saṅghabhadra, who was born in a western country but educated in Ceylon, came to China with his teacher, a Tripitak-Acharyya, and translated Buddhaghosa's *Sāmantapasadika* in A.D. 488. In the 6th century there was a continued development of the maritime intercourse between India and China. In the year 526 A.D. Bodhidharma, the great patriarch of Indian Buddhism, who was the son of a king of Southern India, embarked in his old age from India, and "reached Canton by sea." He was received with the honour due to his age and character, and invited to Nanking, where the Emperor of South China held his court. As the Chinese geographer, Chia-Tau, also records in his *Huang-hua-hsi-ta-chi*, "Ta-mo (i.e. Bodhidharma) came floating on the sea to Pan-yu (i.e. Canton)."[1] The arrival of Bodhidharma gave a great impetus to Indian missionary activity in China, where it is recorded that there were at work at one time and in one province, viz. Lo-Yang, "more than 3,000 Indian monks and 10,000 Indian families to impress their national religion and art on Chinese soil."[2] Specific mention of individual sea voyages to China also appears in Chinese works. Thus the *Kwai-Yuen Catalogue* records that in A.D. 548 Paramati, who was a native of Ujjaini, being invited by the Emperor Wu, of the Llan dynasty, arrived on the southern coast of China. In the *Suyshoo*, a Chinese history of the Suy dynasty, it is stated that in A.D. 607 the King of Ceylon "sent the Brahman, Kewmo-lo, with 30 vessels to meet the approaching ships which conveyed an embassy from China." Ceylon had at that time a fully developed national marine which, according to the *Mahāwaṅso* (ch. xl.), was founded as early as A.D. 495 by the king Mogallana for the defence of the coast.

---

[1] *J.R.A.S.*, 1896, and Edkins' *Chinese Buddhism*, p. 100.

[2] Okakura's *Ideals of the East*, p. 113.

CHAPTER VIII.

THE PERIOD OF HINDU IMPERIALISM IN NORTHERN INDIA (*continued*): MARITIME ACTIVITY ON THE WEST COAST.

DURING the latter days of the Gupta Empire, i.e. during the 5th and 6th centuries A.D., Indian maritime activity was equally manifest towards the West. In the 5th century, according to Hamza of Ispahan, the ships of India and China could be seen constantly moored at Hira, near Kufa, on the Euphrates.[1] The ports of Sindh and Gujarat appear among the chief centres of this naval enterprise of the time. It was from these ports that the Indian adventurers sailed to colonize Java. In A.D. 526 Cosmas found Sindhu or Debal and Orhet, i.e. Soraṭha or Veraval, as leading places of trade with Ceylon.[2] In the 6th century, apparently driven out by the White Hunas, the Jats from the Indus and Cutch occupied the islands in the Bahrein Gulf. About the same time, as Fergusson has pointed out, Amravati, at the mouth of the Kṛishñā, was superseded as the port for the Golden Chersonese by the accomplishment of the direct voyage from Gujarat and the west coast of India.

---

[1] Yule's *Cathay*, I, lxxviii.

[2] *Ibid.* I, clxxviii.

In the time of the empire of S'rī Harsha, succeeding that of the Guptas, the people of Surastra were described by Hiuen Tsang (about A.D. 630) as deriving their livehood from the sea by engaging in commerce and exchanging commodities.[1] He further notices that in the chief cities of Persia, Hindus were settled enjoying the full practice of their religion.[2] Again, the Jats were probably the moving spirit in the early Mahomedan sea raids (A.D. 630–770) against the Gujarat and Konkan coasts. During the 7th and 8th centuries, when the chief migrations by sea from Gujarat to Java and Cambodia seem to have taken place, Chinese fleets visited Diu under the pilotage probably of the Jats. On the Sindh, Cutch, and Gujarat coasts, besides the Jats there were other tribes that showed notable energy at sea. Thus in the 7th and 8th centuries the Gurjjaras, chiefly of the Chapa or Chavada clan, both in Dwarka and Somnath, and inland, rose to power, and about A.D. 740 established themselves at Anahilavada Patan. They tried to put down the piracy of the Jats, but afterwards themselves became more dangerous pirates.

---

[1] Beal, *Buddhist Records*, vol. ii., p. 269.

[2] Reinaud's *Abulfeda*, ccclxxxv.

CHAPTER IX.

THE PERIOD OF HINDU IMPERIALISM IN SOUTHERN INDIA: THE RISE OF THE CHALUKYAS AND THE CHOLAS—FROM THE MIDDLE OF THE 7TH CENTURY TO THE TIME OF THE MAHOMEDAN CONQUESTS IN NORTHERN INDIA.

THE period succeeding that of the Guptas and Harshavardhana was also equally characterized by remarkable outbursts of naval enterprise and colonizing activity, bringing about a further expansion of India. The field of maritime activity in the Eastern waters was considerably widened. For along with the intercourse of India with China there was developed in this period the intercourse with Japan in the farthest East. As regards the intercourse with China we have fresh facts to record. The *Chu-fan-chih* of Chao Jukua, a Chinese traveller of the 13th century, relates that during the periods Cheng-Kuan (A.D. 627–650) and T'ien-shou (A.D. 690–692) of the T'ang dynasty, the people of T'ien-chu (i.e. India) sent envoys with tribute to China.[1] According to the *Kwai-Yuen Catalogue*, Punya-upachaya, who was a native of Central India, came to China from Ceylon in A.D. 655, while

[1] See *J.R.A.S.*, 1896, p. 490.

Jñana-bhadra, a Buddhist from Palyan of the "Southern Ocean," came to China for the second time after having visited India from China by sea. Some very interesting facts regarding the maritime intercourse between China and India are furnished by the famous Chinese traveller I-Tsing,[1] who visited India in A.D. 673. He has recorded the itineraries of about sixty Chinese pilgrims who visited India in the 7th century A.D., from which it is clear that there was constant traffic across the sea between India and China. The whole coast of Farther India from Suvarṇabhūmi or Burma to China, and also of the islands of the Malay Archipelago, was studded with prosperous Indian colonies and naval stations, which ocean-liners regularly plying in the Eastern waters between India and China constantly used as convenient halting-places. I-Tsing refers to more than ten such colonies where Indian manners, customs, and religious practices prevailed together with Sanskrit learning. These were S'rī-Bhoja in Sumatra, Kalinga in Java, Mahasin in Borneo, and the islands of Bali, Bhojapara, etc., which had all Indian names, and afforded to Chinese pilgrims to India a good preparatory training. In these colonies or naval stations passengers often changed their ship, though many would come direct to

[1] *I-Tsing*, by Dr. Taka-kusu.

Bengal, like I-Tsing, who disembarked at the port of Tamralipti, while others would halt at Ceylon, that sacred place of Buddhism, to re-ship themselves for Bengal, like Fa-Hien. I-Tsing has also recorded the names of some of his contemporaries who like him visited India by way of the sea. One was Tao-lin, the Master of the Law, who came to Tamralipti by way of Java and Nicobars. Another was Ta-tcheng-teng, who came by way of Ceylon and lived at the monastery named Varāha in Tamralipti.

Throughout this period we have also frequent notices in Chinese annals of Indian Buddhist devotees visiting China, as we have those of Chinese Buddhists visiting India with the permission of their emperor. Thus the *Kwai-Yuen Catalogue*, to which we have already referred, mentions the name of the Indian Vajrabodhi, who came to China by sea and entered the capital in A.D. 720 He was born in Malaya, a mountainous district in either Southern India or Ceylon, translated many Mantra texts, and became the founder of Mystical Buddhism in China. The son of an Indian king, Manju Srī by name, a very zealous Buddhist, came to China, but left the royal court through misunderstanding, and went off indignant to the southern coast to embark in a merchant vessel for India. At the time of Yung-hsi (A.D. 984–988) a Buddhist devotee, by name Lo-hu-na, arrived in China by sea; he called himself a native of T'ien-chu (India). In Col. Yule's *Cathay and the Way Thither* we have a record of the various instances of intercourse between China and India from the earliest times downwards, both by sea and land.

As regards the intercourse with Japan, which also developed during this period, we have a few conclusive facts and evidences to adduce. Japanese tradition records the names of Indian evangelists who visited Japan to propagate the Buddhistic faith. Thus Bodhidharma, of South India, after working in China, came to Japan and had an interview with Prince Shotoku (A.D. 573–621). Subkakara was another Indian, a native of Central India, who, while working in China (716–735), privately visited Japan and left at the Kumedera Temple, in the province of Yamato, a book of the *Mahāvairochanabhisambodhi Sutra*, consisting of seven books, the fundamental doctrines of Buddhistic Tantrism.[1] The visit of the Indian missionary, Bodhisena, to Japan in A.D. 736 is a historical fact. Bodhisena had originally gone to China to see a Chinese sage, Manju S'rī, and while staying in a temple there came in contact with a Japanese envoy to the Celestial court, and was

[1] Rev. Daito Shimaji on "India and Japan in Ancient Times," in the *Journal of the Indo-Japanese Association*, January, 1910.

persuaded by the latter to visit Japan. He settled in Japan, and taught Sanskrit to Japanese priests. He was most bountifully provided by the Imperial Court, and most devotedly loved by the populace.

But India contributed not only to the religion of Japan but also to her industry. The official annals of Japan record how eleven centuries ago cotton was introduced into Japan by two Indians. The eighth volume of the *Nihon-Ko-Ki* records how in July, 799, a foreigner was washed ashore in a little boat somewhere on the southern coast of Mikwa Province in Japan. He confessed himself to be a man from "Ten-jiku," as India was then called in Japan. Among his effects was found something like grass-seeds, which proved to be no other than some seeds of the cotton-plant. Again, it is written in the 199th chapter of the *Ruijukokushi* (another official record) that a man from Kuen-lum was cast up on Japanese shores in April, 800, and that the cotton-seeds he had brought with him were sown in the provinces of Kii, Awaji, Sanuki, Jyo, Tosa, and Kyushu. These two records are enough to convince us that cotton was introduced into Japan through the Indians who were unfortunately carried over to that country by the "black current."[1]

Towards the end of the 10th and the early part

[1] Dr. Taka-Kusu on "What Japan Owes to India" in the *Journal of the Indo-Japanese Association*, January, 1910.

of the 11th century, Southern India witnessed a remarkable outburst of naval activity under the strong government of a succession of Chola kings. The first of this line of rulers was Rāja-rāja the Great, who ascended the throne in A.D. 985. He began his career of conquest by the destruction of the Chera fleet in the roads of Kandalur (probably on the west coast), and passed from victory to victory till, in the course of a busy reign of twenty-seven years, he made himself beyond dispute the Lord Paramount of Southern India, ruling a realm which included the whole of the Madras Presidency and a large part of Mysore, together with Kalingam, which he conquered in the sixteenth year of his reign. Ceylon (Ilam) also was added to his empire in the twentieth year, for he built up a powerful navy, and his operations were not confined merely to the land. Rāja-rāja Chola (A.D. 984–1013) was succeeded by his son Rājendra Choladeva I., under whose long and brilliant rule from A.D. 1013 to 1044 the power of the Cholas reached its high-water mark and their empire its widest extent. In inscriptions dated in the twelfth year of his reign (A.D. 1025) he is said to have conquered Orissa, Gujarat, Behar, and Bengal, and reached the banks of the Ganges, for which he assumed the title of Gangaikonda-chola (the Chola who seized the Ganges). In the inscriptions of his thirteenth year detailing his conquests we find that he also conquered "the whole kingdom of Ilam (Ceylon) in the raging ocean girt by the crystal waves of the sea," as well as "countless *old* islands (about 12,000 in number) in the midst of the ocean in which conches resound," which were probably the Laccadives and Maldives. In the same inscription it is also recorded that he achieved a great naval victory over "Saṅgrāma Vijayottunga Varman, the King of Kadaram, whom he caught by dispatching (his army in) many ships across the stormy sea and his huge elephants furious as the roaring sea." This "stormy sea" was no doubt the Bay of Bengal if Kadaram is identified with the ancient kingdom of Prome or Pegu, also known as Tharekhettra. The inscription also describes Kadaram as being "difficult to attack, being defended by the sea." All this, therefore, indicates that the naval power of the Cholas was considerably developed, making itself felt even on the opposite coast of the Bay of Bengal. In addition to Kadaram there were also taken on the same coast the flourishing seaports of Takkolam (the *Takola* of Ptolemy, where, according to the *Indian Antiquary*, vol. xxi., p. 383, "cables, ropes, and other vestiges of sea-going vessels are still frequently dug up") and Matama or Martaban. Then followed the annexation of the whole of the kingdom, which was named S'rī Vishaya and Nakkavaram or the Nicobar and Andaman Islands. These exploits are thus referred to in the Tamil poem *Kalinga Huparani*: "The war-elephants of the Chola drank water of the Ganges at Mannai: and Kadaram, where the roaring crystal waves washed the sand mixed with red gold, was annexed" (canto viii., stanza 25).[1]

The naval activity of the Chola emperors was not, however, confined within the limits of the Bay of Bengal. They appear to have carried on their intercourse with countries of the farther East as far as China. In the *Sungshih*, a Chinese work, the names of the two Chola kings are mentioned who sent embassies with tribute to China, viz.: in A.D. 1033, Shih-li-lo-ch'a-yin-to-lo-chu-lo, i.e. S'rī Rāja Indra Chola; and again in A.D. 1077, Ti-wa-ka-lo, which may stand for the Chola king Kulotunga (A.D. 1077–1118). The last embassy consisted of 72 men; it was probably, like most of the missions to the coast of China, nothing better than a trading expedition on joint account, the 72 ambassadors being the shareholders or their supercargoes.[2]

---

[1] The authorities consulted for the Chola history are V. Kanakasabhai's articles on "Rāja-Rāja Chola," "The Conquest of Bengal and Burma by the Tamils," and S. Krishnaswami Aiyangar's article on "The Chola Ascendancy in Southern India," in the *Madras Review* for 1902, vol. viii.

[2] *J.R.A.S.*, 1896, pp. 490 ff.

CHAPTER X.

RETROSPECT.

WE have now set forth at some length the available evidences bearing on the history of the shipping, sea-borne trade, and maritime activity of India from the earliest times down to the period of the Musalman conquests in Northern India. We have considered the kind of maritime activity and commerce which India had in the long and ancient period before the Mauryan in the light of the evidences from both literary works and archaeological finds, and are quite prepared for the remarkable outburst of naval activity and growth of foreign intercourse which has been established beyond doubt or dispute to be the characteristic of the Mauryan period. We have next seen how the impetus given to the development of India's international life under the Mauryan Empire in the days of Chandra Gupta and Asoka survived that empire itself and continued to gain in force and volume amid the vicissitudes of her domestic politics. Dynasty after dynasty succeeded to the position of paramount power in the land, but the course of commerce ran smooth through all these changes. The opening centuries of the Christian era, which saw the political unity of India divided by the Kushans of the north and the Andhras of the south, with the Vindhyas as their mutual boundary, were also, as we have seen, the period of a remarkable growth of foreign commerce, especially with Rome, that was shared equally by the north and the south. This is shown, on the one hand, unmistakably by the books of Roman writers with their remarkably accurate details regarding Indian exports and imports, ports, and harbours, and, on the other hand, by the unimpeachable testimony of many finds of Roman coins both in Northern and Southern India.

A consideration of the kind of things which India sent abroad in exchange for the things she imported and a glance at the list of Indian exports and imports, such as that given in that most interesting work on Oriental commerce, the *Periplus of the Erythraean Sea*, will reveal certain peculiar features regarding the economical system of ancient India, to which has been traced the proverbial "wealth of Ind" by many scholars. As remarked by Major J. B. Keith, in a recent article in the *Asiatic Quarterly Review* (July, 1910), "the old prosperity of India was based on the sound principle, which is, that after clothing and feeding your own people, then of your surplus abundance give to the stranger." For it will appear that the chief items of Indian export were the "renowned art industrial fabrics, and exports were not multiplied on the reprehensible practice of depleting a country of its food-stuffs." The result was the development of an external trade to which we owe, on the one hand, the great cities like Baalbek and Palmyra in the desert, and, on the other hand, "those great monuments of art which India was enabled to erect after clothing and feeding her own people." And of the many satrapies of Darius India was also, as we have seen, the only one which could afford to pay her tribute in gold to him. Finally, we should not miss the point of Pliny's famous complaint about allowing India to find a market for her superfluous manufactured luxuries in Rome and thereby suck out her wealth and drain her of gold.

It may also be noted in passing that it was her wonderful achievements in applied chemistry more than her skill in handicraft which enabled India to command for more than a thousand years (from Pliny to Tavernier) the markets of the East as well as the West, and secured to her an easy and universally recognized pre-eminence among the nations of the world in exports and manufactures. Some of the Indian discoveries in chemical arts and manufactures are indicated as early as the 6th century A.D. by Varahamihira in the *Vrihat-Sañhitā.* Thus he mentions several preparations of cements or powders called Vajralepa, "cements strong as the thunderbolt," for which there was ample use in the temple architecture of the times, whose remains still testify to the adamantine strength of these metal or rock cements. Varāhamihira also alludes to the experts in machinery and the professional experts in the composition of dyes and cosmetics, and even artificial imitations of natural flower-scents which bulked so largely in the Indian exports to Rome. Broadly speaking, there were three great discoveries in applied chemistry to which India owed her capture of the world markets, viz. (1) the preparation of fast dyes for textile fabrics by the treatment of natural dyes like *manjishtha* with alum and other chemicals; (2) the extraction of the principle of indigotin from the indigo plant by a process "which, however crude, is essentially an anticipation of modern chemical methods"; and (3) the tempering of steel "in a manner worthy of advanced metallurgy, a process to which the mediaeval world owed its Damascus swords."[1]

Besides the Roman trade, and the trade with the West generally, there was also developed along with it a trade with the East. The West alone could not absorb the entire maritime activity of India, which found another vent in a regular traffic in the Eastern waters between Bengal and Ceylon, Kalinga,

[1] Brajendranath Seal, M.A., Ph.D., in his learned thesis on "The Chemical Theories of the Ancient Hindus."

and Suvarṇabhūmi, and a complete navigation, in fact, of the Bay of Bengal and the Indian Ocean. This Eastern maritime enterprise reached its climax in the age of the Gupta emperors, when India once more, as in the days of Chandra Gupta and Asoka, asserted herself as a dominant factor in Asiatic politics, and even showed symptoms of a colonizing activity that culminated in the civilization of Java, Sumatra, and Cambodia, and laid the foundation of a Greater India. Towards the later days of the Gupta Empire, Indian maritime activity in the Eastern waters had a vastly extended field, embracing within its sphere not only Farther India and the islands of the Indian Archipelago, but also China, with which a regular and ceaseless traffic by way of the sea was established and long continued. Lastly, we find the sphere of this Eastern naval activity widening still further during the days of Harshavardhana and Pulakeshi, the Chalukyas and the Cholas, till Japan in the farthest East is brought within the range of Indian influence, and becomes the objective of Indian missionary and colonizing activity.

BOOK II. MAHOMEDAN PERIOD.

BOOK II.—MAHOMEDAN PERIOD.

CHAPTER I.

THE PRE-MOGUL PERIOD.

WE shall now briefly narrate the history of Indian maritime enterprise after the advent and conquests of the Musalmans.

We begin first with the history of Sindh, and particularly of its Arab conquests, which furnishes many instances of Indian naval activity and enterprise. The immediate cause of the Arab conquests was the exaction of vengeance for the plunder, by the Meds and other pirates of Debal and the Indus mouths, of eight vessels, which the ruler of Ceylon had dispatched, fitted with presents, pilgrims, Mahomèdan orphans, and Abyssinian slaves, to secure the good-will of Hajjaj and the Khalif[1] in the 8th century (A.D. 712). It will be remembered that these Indian pirates had been carrying on their activities from very early times. They inspired with alarm the Persian

---

[1] *Al-Biladuri* in Elliot, vol. i., p. 118; also Appendix, p. 429.

monarchy even in the days of its most absolute power. According to Strabo and Arrian it was to protect their cities against these piratical attacks that the Persians made the Tigris entirely inaccessible for navigation, till Alexander, on his return from India, to further commercial intercourse caused to be removed the masses of stone by which the course of the stream was obstructed. It has also been supposed that, inspired by the same dread, and not from religious motives, the Persians built no city of any note upon the sea-coast.[1]

Muhammad ibn Kasim, the Arab conqueror of Sindh, arrived at Debal in ships carrying his men, arms, and warlike machines, one of which, the *manjanik*, required 500 men to work it.[2] He had also to construct bridges of boats in order to effect his passage of the rivers of Sindh.[3]

From the 9th century we get notices of India by the Arabs. The commerce of the Arabs was at its highest activity under the Caliphs of Bagdad, under whom the Arabs conquered Egypt, closed Alexandria to Europeans, and founded Bussora (A.D. 635) at the head of the Persian Gulf, rivalling Alexandria as the centre of the Eastern trade. The voyages of Sindabad the Sailor belong to the 9th century.

---

[1] See Elliot, vol. i., p. 513.

[2] *Al-Biladuri* in Elliot, vol. i., p. 120.

[3] *Chach-nama* in Elliot, vol. i., p. 167.

About A.D. 851 Suleiman, a merchant of Bussorah, speaks of the Sea of Lar (which washes Gujarat and Malabar), of Serendip or Ceylon, and the like. Masudi of Bagdad (A.D. 890–956) visited India, and mentions nutmegs, cloves, camphor, and sandal-wood as Indian products.[1]

In the 11th century, according to the *Tabakat-i-Akbari* of Nizamuddin Ahmed, the 17th expedition of Sultan Mahmud was directed against the Jats who had molested his army on his return from Somnath. It was a brilliant naval fight, and is thus described by the historian :—

> He led a large force towards Multan, and when he arrived there he ordered 1,400 boats to be built, each of which was armed with three firm iron spikes, projecting one from the prow and two from the sides, so that everything which came in contact with them would infallibly be destroyed. In each boat were 20 archers, with bows and arrows, grenades, and naphtha, and in this way proceeded to attack the Jats, who, having intelligence of the armament, sent their families into the islands and prepared themselves for the conflict. They launched, according to some, 4,000 boats, and according to others 8,000 boats, manned and armed, ready to engage the Mahammadans. Both fleets met, and a desperate conflict ensued. Every boat of the Jats that approached the Moslem fleet, when it received the shock of the projecting spikes, was broken and overturned. Thus, most of the Jats were drowned, and those who were not so destroyed were put to the sword.[2]

Al-Biruni gives some interesting details regarding the Indian maritime and commercial activity of the 11th century. He has referred to the pirates

---

[1] Sir G. Birdwood in his *Report on the Old Records of the India Office.*

[2] Elliot, vol. ii., p. 478.

infesting the western coast, named Bawarij, who are so called because "they commit their depredations in boats called Baira." [1]

The coasts of Gujarat were the scene of much commercial activity, from which sugar from Malwa, badru (bam) and baladi were exported in ships to all countries and cities.[2]

Malabar also was in those days the "Key of Hind," whose productions, such as rubies, aromatics, grasses, and pearls, were "carried to Irak, Khurasan, Syria, Rum, and Europe." It has also a great amount of *entrepôt* trade, for "large ships, called in the language of China 'junks,' bring various sorts of choice merchandise and cloths from China and Machin, and the countries of Hind and Sindh." [3] Wassaf (A.D. 1328) speaks of these junks as sailing like mountains with the wings of the winds on the surface of the water.

In the 12th century, Al-Idrisi found Debal to be a "station for the vessels of Sindh and other countries," whither came the "vessels of China and ships laden with the productions of Uman." Baruh (Broach) was a port for the vessels coming from China, as also for those of Sindh.[4] He also mentions the cotton fabrics of Coromandel, the

---

[1] "Rashiuddin from Al-Biruni," in Sir H. Elliot's *History of India*, vol. i., p. 65.

[2] *Ibid.*, p. 67. [3] *Ibid.*, p. 69. [4] *Ibid.*, pp. 77, 87.

pepper and cardamomes of Malabar, and the lemons of Mansura on the " Mehran " (Indus).[1] Again, in the 12th century, intercourse with the farther East is proved by the fact that Gupta (A.D. 319–500) and White Huna (A.D. 500–580) coins were said to have been in use in Madagascar and the islands of the Malaya Archipelago,[2] and, according to Abul-Feda, the merchants of Java could understand the language of the natives of Madagascar.[3]

In the 13th century an important naval expedition was directed by Ghiyas-ud-din Balban (1266–86 A.D.) against Tughril Khan, Governor of Bengal, who declared himself independent of Delhi, and assumed royal insignia. Two previous attempts to subdue him having failed, the Sultan " resolved to march against the rebel in person, and ordered a large number of boats to be collected on the Ganges and the Jumna. . . . Proceeding into Oudh, he ordered a general levy, and two lakhs of men of all classes were enrolled. An immense fleet of boats was collected, and in these he passed his army over the Sarau (the Saraju or Gogra). The rains now came on, and, although he had plenty of boats, the passage through the low-lying country was difficult." Tughril fled from Lakhnauti to Jajnagar (some-

---

[1] Sir George Birdwood in his *Report on the Old Records of the India Office.*

[2] Reinaud's *Mémoires*, p. 236. [3] Reinaud's *Abulfeda*, ch. xxii.

where near modern Tiperrah). Balban marched from Lakhnauti in pursuit of the rebel with all speed, and in a few days arrived at Sunar-gnaw. The Rai of that place, by name Danuj Rai, met the Sultan, and an agreement was made with him that he should guard against the escape of Tughril by water. The expedition ended in the death of Tughril, and the complete defeat of his army, and "such punishment as was inflicted on Lakhnauti had never been heard of in Delhi, and no one could remember anything like it in Hindusthan."[1]

The foreign travellers who visited India towards the latter part of the same century were Abulfeda of Damascus and the famous Marco Polo. Abulfeda (A.D. 1273–1331) mentions the pepper of Malabar and the fine cotton manufactures of Coromandel. Marco Polo (A.D. 1292) found the Coromandel coast a great centre of pearl-fishing, and the Gujarat coast of desperate piracy. These pirates sailed every year with their wives and children in more than a hundred corsair vessels, staying out the whole summer. They are also said to have joined in fleets of twenty to thirty, and made a sea cordon five or six miles apart. Marco Polo also found Sokotra a prey to multitudes of Hindu pirates who encamped there and sold off their booty. He also mentions *Cail* (Kayal in the Tinnevelly dis-

[1] Barni's *Tarikh-i-Firozshahi*, in Elliot, vol. iii., pp. 115–121.

trict) as the city where "all the ships touch that come from the West . . . laden with horses and other things for sale." Of Coilum (Quilon) he says, "a great deal of brazil is got here, also ginger and pepper, and very fine indigo. The merchants from Arabia and Persia come hither with their ships." He speaks of Tana (Thana) "where grow no pepper or spices, but plenty of incense. There is much traffic here and many ships and merchants frequent the place, for there is a great export of leather and buckram and cotton." Of Cambaet (Cambay) he says, "it produces indigo in plenty, and much fine buckram; cotton is exported hence; there is a great trade in *hides, which are very well dressed.*" He speaks of Aden as a "port to which many ships of India come with their cargoes." He also mentions Indian vessels sailing as far as the island of Zanguebar, which they took twenty days in reaching from Coromandel, but three months in returning, "so strong does the current lie towards the south."

Marco Polo has also left some very important and interesting details regarding Indian ships which are well worth a notice. According to him, the ships that are employed in navigation are built of fir-timber; they are all doubled-planked, that is, they have a course of sheathing boards laid over the planking in every part. These are caulked with oakum both within and without, and are fastened with iron nails. The bottoms are smeared over with a preparation of quicklime and hemp, pounded together and mixed with oil procured from a certain tree, which makes a kind of unguent that "retains its viscous properties more firmly and is a better material than pitch."

Besides the construction of Indian ships, Marco Polo gives details regarding their size, form, and fittings, and the mode of repairing. He saw ships of so large a size as to require a crew of 300 men, and other ships that were manned by crews of 200 and 150 men. These ships could carry from five to six thousand baskets (or mat bags) of pepper, a fact which indicates to some extent the tonnage of these Indian vessels. These ships were moved with oars or sweeps, and each oar required four men to work it. They were usually accompanied by two or three large barks with a capacity to contain one thousand baskets of pepper, and requiring a crew of sixty, eighty, or one hundred sailors. These small craft were often employed to tow the larger vessels, when working their oars, or even under sail, provided, of course, the wind be on the quarter, and not when right aft, because in that case the sails of the larger vessel must becalm those of the smaller, which would in consequence be run down. Besides these barks, these ships carried with them as many as ten small boats for the purpose of carrying out anchors, for fishing, and a variety of other services.

As in modern steamers and ocean-liners, these boats were slung over the sides of the main ship and lowered into the water when there was occasion to use them. The barks also were in like manner provided with their smaller boats. The larger vessel had usually a single deck, and below the deck the space was divided into sixty small cabins, fewer or more according to the size of vessel, and each cabin afforded accommodation for one merchant. It was also provided with a good helm, with four masts, and as many sails. Some ships of the larger class had, besides the cabins, as many as thirteen bulkheads or divisions in the hold, formed of thick planks let into each other (*incastrati*, mortised or rabbeted). The object of these was to guard against accidents which might make the vessel spring a leak, such as "striking on a rock or receiving a stroke from a whale." For if water chanced to run in, it could not, in consequence of the boards being so well fitted, pass from one division to another, and the goods might be easily removed from the division affected by the water. In case of a ship needing repair, the practice was to give her a course of sheathing over the original boarding, thus forming a third course, and this, if she needed further repairs, was repeated even to the number of six layers, after which she was condemned as unserviceable and not seaworthy.

Marco Polo has also left a very interesting

description of the pearl-fishings of Malabar. It was conducted by a number of merchants who formed themselves into several companies, and employed many vessels and boats of different sizes, well provided with ground-tackle by which to ride safely at anchor. They engaged and carried with them persons who were skilled in the art of diving for the oysters in which the pearls were enclosed. These the divers brought up in bags made of netting that were fastened about their bodies, and then repeated the operation, rising to the surface when they could no longer keep their breath, and after a short interval diving again.[1]

In the 14th century, we have in the account of the voyage across the Indian Ocean of Friar Odoric[2] (A.D. 1321), in a ship that carried full 700 people, a striking proof of the capacity and maritime skill of the Rajput sailors of Gujarat; who could successfully manage such large vessels.[3] There is even an earlier mention of Rajput ships sailing between Sumena (Somnaṭh) and China in Yule's *Cathay*. To the same century belonged Ibn Batuta, the greatest Arab traveller,

---

[1] *The Travels of Marco Polo* (Marsden's Translation), ed. Thomas Wright.

[2] Dr. Vincent remarks : "This is a confirmation of the account we have of those large ships from the time of Agatharcides down to the 16th century ; the ships of Guzarat which traversed the Indian Ocean in all ages."

[3] Stevenson, in *Kerr's Voyages*, xviii. 324.

who spent twenty-four years (A.D. 1325–1349) in travelling. Being sent by Muhammad Tughlak on an embassy to China, he embarked from Cambay, and after many adventures at Calicut, Ceylon and Bengal he at last took his passage toward China in a junk bound for "Java," as he called it, but in fact Sumatra. Returning from China, he sailed direct from the coast of Malabar to Muscat and Ormuz. He confirms the statement of Marco Polo regarding the maritime and piratical habits of the Malabar people, who, however, captured only those vessels which attempted to pass their ports without the payment of toll.

Wassaf, in the same century, speaks of the large importation of Arab and Persian horses to Malabar, which in the reign of Abu Bakr even reached the modest figure of 10,000 horses every year.[1] This horse trade was also noticed by Marco Polo (A.D. 1308), who remarks that "the greater part of the revenue of the country is employed in obtaining the horses from foreign countries."[2] Wassaf also notices the *entrepôt* trade of Malabar by which the produce of remotest China was consumed in the farthest West.[3]

In Northern India, in A.D. 1353 and A.D. 1360,

---

[1] Elliot, vol. iii., pp. 28, 32, 33.

[2] *Travels*, Murray's Edition, p. 296.

[3] Elliot, vol. iii., p. 35.

two expeditions were directed against Lakhnauti by Sultan Firoz Shah Tuglak, in both of which "many barrier-breaking boats (*kistiha-i-bandkushan*) were used, in which his whole army, consisting of a lac of troops, had to embark in crossing rivers round the islands of Ekdala and Sunar-gnaw."[1] In A.D. 1372, with an army consisting of 90,000 cavalry and 480 elephants, Firoz Shah led an expedition against Thatta, in which he collected and used a fleet of as many as 5,000 boats, in which the army descended the River Indus and in a few days reached Thatta.[2]

In A.D. 1388 Timur crossed the mighty river of the Indus by means of a bridge of boats constructed in the short space of two days; afterwards he marched to capture the island of Shahabuddin in the River Jhelum, though Shahabuddin effected his escape down the river in 200 boats. Shahabuddin's fleet of boats was, however, completely destroyed near Multan. Timur again had to fight several naval battles on the Ganges. On one occasion he had to encounter a force of Hindus coming down the river in 48 boats, which afterwards fell into his hands.[3]

After Marco Polo, the most important foreign notice of India is the account of Mahuan,[4] the

---

[1] *Tarikh-i-Firozshahi*, in Elliot, vol. iii., pp. 293 ff.

[2] *Ibid.*, pp. 321–322.

[3] *Malfuzat-i-Timuri*, in Elliot, vol. iii., pp. 408–12, 453.

[4] George Phillips in the *J.R.A.S.*, 1896, pp. 204 ff.

Mahomedan Chinaman, who was attached as interpreter to the suite of Cheng-Ho when he made his voyages to India and other places at the beginning of the 15th century. He describes Calicut (A.D. 1409) as a great emporium of trade, frequented by merchants from all quarters, and says "when a ship arrives from China the King's Overseers, with a *chitti* (capitalist), go on board and make an invoice of the goods, and a day is fixed for valuing the cargo." According to Mahuan, the *Ming-shih*, or history of the Ming dynasty, records that Ai-ya-sei-ting (Ghiyas-ud-din Azam Shah, who reigned A.D. 1385–1457), the King of Pang-Kola, sent to the Chinese court in 1408 an embassy with presents including horses and saddles, gold and silver ornaments, drinking vessels of white porcelain with azure flowers, and many other things; and that in 1409 the same king, called Gai-ya-syu-ting, sent another embassy to China. In A.D. 1412 the Chinese ambassador of the return embassy met Indian envoys bringing the usual presents, and learnt from them that the king had died and had been succeeded by Saifuting (Saif-ud-din Hamza Shah, 1407–10). According to Chinese annals he, too, sent an embassy to the Chinese emperor, with a letter written on gold-leaf, and presenting a giraffe. This embassy arrived in China in the 12th year of Yung-lo, A.D. 1415. In this year also a Chinese embassy under Prince Tsi-chao, with presents, was received by the Bengal king, his queen and ministers.[1] Thus, in the first half of the 15th century, an active sea-borne trade and commercial intercourse were going on between Bengal and China; and the silver money of Bengal used at this period to be called Tung-kia, weighing about 163·24 grains.

For the 15th century Abd-er-Razzak[2] (A.D. 1442) has left a highly interesting account of the important harbour of Calicut, which is regarded as "one of the greatest shipping centres of the world in this period." Says he:—

> From Calicut are vessels continually sailing for Mecca, which are for the most part laden with pepper. The inhabitants of Calicut are adventurous sailors, and pirates do not dare to attack the vessels of Calicut. In this harbour one may find everything that can be desired.

Again:—

> Security and justice are so firmly established in this city that the most wealthy merchants bring thither from maritime countries considerable cargoes, which they unload, and unhesitatingly send into the markets and the bazaars, without thinking in the meantime of any necessity of checking the account or of keeping watch over the goods. The officers of the custom-house take upon themselves the charge of looking after the merchandise, over which they keep watch day and night. When a sale is effected they levy a duty on the goods of one-fortieth part; if they are not sold they make no charge on them whatsoever. In other parts a strange practice is adopted. When a vessel sets sail for a certain point, and suddenly is driven by a decree of Divine Providence into another roadstead, the inhabitants, under the pretext that the wind has driven it there, plunder the ship. But at Calicut, every ship, whatever place it may come from, or wherever it may be bound, when it puts into this port is treated like other vessels, and has no trouble of any kind to put up with.

---

[1] George Phillips in the *J.R.A.S.*, 1896, pp. 204 ff.

[2] *India in the Fifteenth Century* (Hakluyt Society's publication), i. 14, i. 19.

Nicolo Conti[1] was another traveller in the earlier part of the 15th century who gives some interesting details regarding Indian shipbuilding and commerce. Thus he says: "The natives of India build some ships *larger than ours*, capable of containing 2,000 butts, and with five sails and as many masts. The lower part is constructed with triple planks, in order to withstand the force of the tempests to which they are much exposed. But some ships are so built in compartments that should one part be shattered, the other portion remaining entire may accomplish the voyage." On the banks of the Ganges he was astonished to see bamboos growing supremely high and thick, of which "fishing boats are made and skiffs adapted to the navigation of the river." Of the Indian merchants of the south he makes a wonderful statement which deserves to be carefully noted: "They are very rich, so much so that some will carry on their business *in forty of their own ships, each of which is valued at* 15,000 *gold pieces*."

Hieronimo di Santo Stefano,[2] a Genoese merchant, visited India on a mercantile speculation at the close of the 15th century. He embarked from Cosir (Cairo) "on board a ship, the timbers of which were sewn together with cords and the sails

[1] *India in the Fifteenth Century* (Hakluyt Society's publication), ii. 10, 21, 27.

[2] *Ibid.*, iv. 4, 8, 9.

made of cotton." While sailing from Sumatra in a ship to return to Cambay he was wrecked in a storm off the Maldives, and was floating on a large plank of wood when "three ships which had parted from our company and had been five miles in advance of us, learning our disaster, immediately sent out their boats . . . and I arrived in one of the said ships at Cambay."

Of the 15th and the earlier part of the 16th century there are other facts to show that much of the Indian maritime activity was manifested on the western coast. Till the arrival of the Portuguese (A.D. 1500–1508) the Ahmedabad sultans maintained their position as lords of the sea.[1] At this time Java appears in the State list of foreign bandars which paid tribute, the tribute being probably a cess or ship-tax paid by the Gujarat traders with Java in return for the protection of the royal navy.[2] In 1429 the Gujarat king Ahmad Shah sent a fleet of seventeen vessels to recover the Island of Bombay and Salsette seized by the Bahmani kingdom. Between 1453–1469 the Raja of Vishalgad, one of the coast fortresses, built up a great maritime power, and with a fleet of 300 vessels began to harass the commerce of the Musalmans till he was

---

[1] When in A.D. 1535 he secured Bahadur's splendid jewelled belt, Humayun said: "These are the equipments of the lord of the sea." See Bayley's *Gujarat*, 386.

[2] Bird's *Gujarat*, 131.

subdued by treachery by the King of Gujarat. Mahmud, probably the greatest of the kings of Gujarat (A.D. 1459–1511), organized and maintained a large fleet to subdue the pirates that infested his coasts.[1] In East Africa in A.D. 1498 Vasco de Gama found sailors from Cambay and other parts of India, who guided themselves by the help of the stars in the north and south, and had nautical instruments of their own (*J.A.S.B.*, vol. v., p. 784). Again, in A.D. 1510 Albuquerque found a strong Hindu element in Java and Malacca, and Sumatra ruled by a Hindu named Parameshwara. In A.D. 1508 the Gujarat fleet combined with the Egyptian to destroy the Portuguese fleet off the harbour of Chaul. In A.D. 1521 the admiral of the King of Gujarat defeated the Portuguese off Chaul and sank one of their vessels. In 1527 another Gujarat fleet was sent to Chaul, but a great number of the ships were destroyed. In 1528 there was a decisive battle off Bandru, in which the Portuguese took 73 ships out of the 80 which composed the Cambay fleet.[2] In 1546 there was another naval battle fought off Diu between the Portuguese, who equipped a large fleet consisting of over 90 sails, and Coje Zofar, a Turk, who was one of the King of Cambay's captains.[3]

---

[1] Elphinstone's *History of India*, Appendix on Gujarat.

[2] *Bombay Gazetteer*, vol. i., Part ii., pp. 29–34, 46.

[3] *Portuguese in India*, by Danvers, pp. 468–74.

In 1584 the Portuguese were defeated in a regular expedition which they sent against the pirates of Goa, then a nest of buccaneers who were organized into a formidable force under the Samurai, practising guerilla warfare and preying on all sea-borne traffic.[1]

During this period the great commercial marts on the western coast were Chaul and Dabhol, carrying on a large trade with Persia and the Red Sea, by which route the whole of the Indian goods designed for Europe then passed. The next important place was Bassein, situated in the great timber-producing district. Many ships used to load there with timber and carry it to Mecca, where the Turks used it for their fleet. Pyrard says that all the timber required at Goa for building houses and ships came from Bassein. Agashi is also spoken of by Portuguese annalists as a large and rich place with a trade in timber. It had a large dockyard in which ships were built:—

> As showing the equality on which these places stood with Portugal in the art of shipbuilding, it must be mentioned that in 1540 an expedition went from Bassein against Agashi with the sole object of getting possession of a great ship which was just built there and was then ready for launching. The ship was taken, and afterwards made several voyages to Portugal. One of the Surat ships stopped by Sir H. Middleton on its voyage to the Red Sea in 1612 was 153 ft. long, 42 beam 31 deep, and said to be of 1,500 tons burden.[2]

---

[1] Whiteway's *Rise of the Portuguese Power in India*, p. 47.

[2] De Coutto, iv. 99; Orme's *Fragments*, 326; quoted in *Bombay Gazetteer*, vol. i., Part ii., pp. 34–36.

One of the Dabhol ships stopped at the same time by Captain Saris in the Red Sea was "153 feet from stem to stern, breadth 42, height 31, burden 1,200 tons; the mainmast 108 feet, the mainyard 132. The English ships of that age (1611) were 300 or 350 tons at most."[1]

Calicut also in the 16th century developed into a great shipping centre. The foreign traveller Varthema has left a very interesting record of shipbuilding in Calicut, giving details about the materials and parts of ships, their names, and the time of navigation, from which we make the following extract:—

> First they make their vessels, such as are open, each of 300 or 400 butts. And when they build the said vessels they do not put any oakum between one plank and another in any way whatever, but they join the planks so well that they keep out the water most excellently. And then they lay on pitch outside, and put in an immense quantity of iron nails. Do not imagine, however, that they have not any oakum, for it comes there in great abundance from other countries, but they are not accustomed to use it for ships. They also possess as good timbers as ourselves and in greater quantity than with us. The *sails* of these ships of theirs are made of cotton, and at the foot of the said sails they carry another sail, and they spread this when they are sailing in order to catch more wind; so that they carry two sails where we carry only one. They also carry *anchors* made of marble, i.e. a piece of marble eight *palmi* long and two *palmi* every other way. The said marble has two large ropes attached to it, and these are the anchors. . . . *The time of their navigation* is this: From Persia to the Cape of Comerin, eight days' voyage from Calicut towards the south. You can navigate through eight months in the year, i.e. September to April; from May to August the sea is very stormy. . . . As to *the names of their ships*, some are called *Sambuchi*, and these are flat-bottomed. Some others, which are made like ours, that is in the

---

[1] *Purchas*, i. 349–350; Dr. Vincent's *Commerce of the Ancients*, vol. ii., p. 38.

bottom, they call *Capel.* Some other quick ships are called *Paroo,* and they are boats of ten paces each, and are all of one piece, and go with oars made of cane, and the mast also is made of cane. There is also another kind of vessel which goes with a sail and oars. These are all made of one piece, of the length of twelve or thirteen paces each. The opening is so narrow that one man cannot sit by the side of the other, but one is obliged to go before the other. They are sharp at both ends. These ships are called *Chaturi,* and go either with a sail or oars more swiftly than any galley, *fusta,* or brigantine.[1]

---

[1] *Travels of Varthema,* edited by G. P. Badger (Hakluyt Society), pp. 152 ff.

MAHOMEDAN PERIOD

CHAPTER II.

The Mogul Period: The Reign of Akbar.

We now reach the age of the Moguls, under whom the political unity of India was nearly attained after the lapse of centuries, and an imperial naval establishment was founded and maintained, especially in Bengal, the home of Indian shipbuilding.

Previous to Akbar we have hardly any record of Indian naval activity except perhaps the two exploits of Babar, the one in A.D. 1528, when Babar fought a naval battle on the Ganges near Kanauj, in which he seized about thirty or forty of the enemy's boats, and the other achieved on the Gogra, on which the army of Kharid collected 100–150 vessels and gave Babar battle.

The government of India under Akbar, however, as might be naturally expected, gave a great impetus to Indian shipping and shipbuilding, especially in Bengal. The main source of our information is of course the *Ayeen-i-Akbari*, that well-known storehouse of accurate details regarding the life and work of Akbar the Great. According to Abul-Fazl, there were framed elaborate regulations for the organization of the Naval Department or Admiralty, the "office of *Meer Behry*" as it was called. These regulations will be found to be remarkably akin to, and in some respects will be even thought to have been anticipated by, the regulations governing Chandra Gupta's Admiralty about 1,900 years earlier, which have been, as we have already seen, preserved for us in that monumental Sanskrit work, the *Arthaśāstra* of Kautilya.

Akbar's Admiralty had, broadly speaking, *four functions* to perform. The *first* was to see to the *supply of ships and boats* for the purpose of navigation, and supervise their building. Vessels were built of various sizes and for various purposes. There were those built for the transportation of elephants, and those of such construction as to be employed in sieges, while others were meant for the conveyance of merchandise. There were also ships which served for convenient habitations. The Emperor had also pleasure-boats built with convenient apartments, and others on which there were floating markets and flower-gardens. Every part of Akbar's empire abounded in ships, but the chief centres of shipbuilding were Bengal, Cashmeer, and Tata. In Allahabad and Lahore also were constructed ships of a size suitable for sea voyages. Along the coasts of the ocean in the west, east, and south of India also, large ships were built which were suitable for voyages.

The *second* duty of Akbar's Admiralty was regarding the *supply of men*, of efficient mariners who knew the nature of tides, the depths of channels, the coasts to be avoided, and the character of the prevailing winds. Every ship required officers and men of the following titles and descriptions: (1) The *Nakhoda*, or commander of the vessel, who directed the course of the ship; (2) the *Maullim* (the mate), who knew the soundings, the situation of the stars, and guided the ship safe to her destination; (3) the *Tundeil*, who was the chief of the *khelasses* or sailors; (4) the *Nakhoda-khesheb*, whose duty it was to provide fuel for the people and assist in lading and unlading the ship; (5) the *Sirheng*, who had to superintend the docking and launching of the ship; (6) the *Bhandaree*, who had charge of the ship's store; (7) the *Keranee*, or ship's clerk, who kept the accounts and also served out water to the people; (8) the *Sukangeer*, or helmsman, of whom there were sometimes twenty in a ship; (9) the *Punjeree*, whose duty it was to look out from the top of the mast and give notice when he saw land or a ship, or discovered a storm rising, or any other object worth observing; (10) the *Goomtee*, or those particular *khelasses* who threw the water out of the ship; (11) the *gunners*, who differed in number according to the size of the ship; (12) the *Kherwah*, or common seamen, who were employed in setting and furling the sails and in stopping leaks, and in case of the anchor sticking fast in the ground they had to go to the bottom of the water to set it free.

The *third* task of the Admiralty was "to watch the rivers," for which an active, resolute man was appointed, who settled everything relative to the ferries, regulated the tonnage, and provided travellers with boats on the shortest notice. Those who were not able to pay at the ferries passed over *gratis*, but no one was permitted to swim across a river. It was also the duty of this officer to hinder boats from travelling in the night except in cases of necessity. Nor was he to allow goods to be landed anywhere except at the public wharfs. Altogether the functions of this officer very nearly corresponded to those of Chandra Gupta's नावध्यक्ष or Superintendent of Ships.

The *fourth* duty of the Admiralty was in regard to the imposition, realization, and remission of duties. Akbar is said to have remitted duties equal to the revenues of a kingdom. Nothing was exacted upon exports and imports excepting a trifle taken at the ports which never exceeded 2½ per cent., and was regarded by merchants as a perfect remission.[1]

The *Ayeen-i-Akbari*[2] also gives some details regarding the *river tolls* in Akbar's time :—

For every boat was charged R. 1 per *kos* at the rate of 1,000 *mans* provided the boat and the men belong to one and the same owner. But if the boat belongs to another man and everything in the boat to the man

---

[1] *Ayeen-i-Akbari*, Gladwin's translation, pp. 193 ff.

[2] Blochmann's translation.

who has hired it, the tax is R. 1 for every 2½ *kos*. At ferry places an elephant has to pay 10*d*. for crossing; a laden cart, 4*d*.; ditto, empty, 2*d*.; a laden camel, 1*d*.; empty camels, horses, cattle with thin things, ½*d*.; ditto, empty, ¼*d*. Other beasts of burden pay 1/16*d*., which included the toll due by the driver. Twenty people pay 1*d*. for crossing, but they are often taken gratis.[1]

As regards details relating to the development of shipping in Bengal, we have to refer to the abstract of *Ausil Toomar Jumma*[2] (original established revenue) of Bengal as settled in behalf of the Mogul Emperor Akbar, about the year 1582, by Raja Todar Mall, in which we find specific assignments for naval establishment. Some *perganas* were definitely assigned for maintaining the Imperial Nowwara (flotilla). Under the head of Omleh Nowwara we have mention of a naval establishment consisting, at the time it was established by Akbar, of 3,000 vessels or boats, but it was afterwards reduced to 768 armed cruisers and boats, besides the number of vessels required to be furnished by the zemindars in return for the lands they held as *jaigeer*. The whole expense of manning the fleet, including the wages of 923 Fringuan or Portuguese sailors, was estimated at Rs. 29,282 monthly, which, with constructing new vessels and repairing the old, amounted annually to Rs. 8,43,452. The fleet was

---

1 Blochmann's translation.

2 See Grant's "Analysis of the Finances of Bengal," in the *Fifth Report of the Select Committee on the Affairs of the East India Company*, vol. i., pp. 245, 246, 270; and Taylor's *Topography of Dacca*, p. 194.

principally stationed at Dacca, as its headquarters, from which was performed its functions for guarding the coast of Bengal against the then very frequent incursions of the Maggs and other foreign pirates or invaders. Under the royal jurisdiction of the Nowwara or Admiralty of Dacca was placed the whole coast from Mundelgaut (near the confluence of the Damodar and Rupnarayan) to the Bundar of Balesore, which was also liable to the invasion of the Maggs. In fact, the ordinary established rental of the whole country was then almost entirely absorbed in jaigeers and protecting the sea-coasts from the ravages of the Maggs or Arrakanese, aided by the Portuguese, who inhabited the port of Chatgaon, and who, in the hope of benefiting through their commerce, had also been allowed to make a settlement at Hugli. The jaigeers that were assigned to the Dacca district for the support of these military establishments of the country were computed to comprise nearly one-third of its extent. The Nowwara jaigeer, which was the principal assignment in the district, included the best lands of the Neabut, and was subdivided into numbers of small Taluks, which were granted to the boatmen and artificers of the fleet.[1] Besides the perganas

[1] *Topography and Statistics of Dacca*, by Taylor (printed by order of Government, 1840).

assigned for the support of the Nowwara, a fruitful source of revenue for the support of the naval establishment was derived from the Mheer Baree, which was a tax on the building of boats varying from 8 as. to R. 1 4 as., according to the size of the vessels. It was levied upon all boats arriving at or leaving the naval headquarters whose crews were not residents of the district.

A boat proceeding to Moorshidabad was charged at the rate of 8 as. per oar; to Calcutta 10 as.; and to Benares R. 1 8 as., while boats arriving from these places were taxed at the rate of 1, 2, and 4 rupees per boat. The Mehal was originally confined to the city, but it afterwards extended to the country, where it was exacted by the zemindars and farmers from every boat that passed their estates. It was considered useful in leading to the detection of dacoits, as a registry of the boats, manjees, and boatmen belonging to each district was kept by the zemindars.[1]

As already pointed out, the naval establishment at Dacca was necessitated by the depredations of the Arrakan pirates, both Magg and Feringi, who used constantly to come by the water route and plunder Bengal. "They carried off the Hindus and Moslems, . . . threw them one above another under the decks of their ships . . . and sold them to the Dutch, English, and French merchants at the ports of the Deccan. Sometimes they brought the captives for sale at a high price to Tamluk and the port of Balasore, which is a part of the imperial

---

[1] Taylor's *Topography of Dacca*, pp. 198, 199.

dominions."[1] With regard to their power it is said that "their cannons are beyond numbering, their flotilla exceeds the waves of the sea."[2] Their ships were so strongly made of timber with a hard core that "cannons could not pierce them."[3] They were such a terror to the Bengal navy that "whenever 100 warships of Bengal sighted four ships of the enemy, if the distance separating them was great the Bengal crew showed fight by flight."[4]

The materials for the building of the Royal Nowwara came from Sylhet, which was then of great importance from its natural growth of ship-timbers, which could be built into vessels of different sizes.[5] The shipyards from the Magg and Feringi fleets were towards the south at Sandwipa, a part of the kingdom of Arrakan. The Venetian traveller, Cesare di Fedrici, writing about the year 1565, states that 200 ships were laden yearly with salt, and that such was the abundance of materials for shipbuilding in this part of the country that the Sultan of Constantinople found it cheaper to have his vessels built here than at Alexandria.[6]

There was quite a large variety of vessels built

---

[1] From the contemporary Persian account of Shihab-ud-din Talish in MS. Bodleian 589, *Sachau and Ethé's Catalogue*, entry 240, translated by Professor Jadunath Sarkar in the *J.A.S.B.* for June, 1907.

[2] *Ibid.* [3] *Ibid.* [4] *Ibid.*

[5] *Fifth Report of the Select Committee*, vol. i., pp. 444–5.

[6] Taylor's *Topography of Dacca*.

and stationed at Dacca. Besides the 768 war-boats making up the Nowwara, there were state-barges for the Viceroys, and two vessels, magnificently fitted up, had annually to be dispatched to the Emperor at Agra, though afterwards, when the Mogul Government declined in vigour, and the Nawabs of Bengal became virtually independent, these state-boats, though avowedly sent for the use of his Majesty, never reached higher than Murshidabad. The state-barges were distinguished by different names according to the figures on their prows, as "Mohrpunkee," from that of a peacock, "Muggurchera," of an alligator, etc. Boating was then a general and favourite pastime with the rich as it was with the Nawabs.[1]

Besides Bengal, the province of Sindh was a great centre of Indian shipping. Abul-Fazl informs us that in the circar of Thatta alone there could be found 40,000 vessels ready for hire.[2] Lahori Bandar in those days was an important seaport on the Indus, and the following account of the harbour regulations in force there given in the *Tarikh-i-Tahiri* is very interesting:—

Between the town of Thatta and Lahori Bandar is a distance of two days' journey, both by land and by water; beyond this it is another day's

---

[1] Taylor's *Topography of Dacca*, pp. 98, 268.

[2] "The means of locomotion is by boats, of which there are many kinds, large and small, to the number of 40,000."—Jarret's translation of the *Ayeen-i-Akbari*, vol. ii., p. 338.

march to the sea. There is a small channel (called *nar* in the language of Thatta) communicating with the port which is unfordable. Between the port and the ocean there is but one inhabited spot, called Suimiani. Here a guard belonging to the Mir Bandar, or port master, with a loaded piece of ordnance, is always stationed. Whenever a ship enters the creek it intimates its approach by firing a gun, which is responded to by the guard-house, in order, by that signal, to inform the people at the port of the arrival of a strange vessel. These, again, instantly send word of its arrival to the merchants of Thatta, and then, embarking on boats, repair to the place where the guard is posted. Ere they reach it, those on the look-out have already inquired into the nature of the ship. Every vessel and trader must undergo this questioning. All concerned in the business now go in their boats (*ghrabs*) to the mouth of the creek. If the ship belong to the port it is allowed to move up and anchor under Lahori Bandar; if it belong to some other part it can go no farther—its cargo is transferred into boats and forwarded to the city.[1]

We may now refer to some of the naval engagements of Akbar's reign. In 1580 Raja Ṭodar Mall, who had been directed to fit out 1,000 boats (*kishti*) and *ghrabs* at Agra, was sent by the Emperor to settle the revenues of Gujarat.[2] In 1590 Akbar sent Khan-i-Khanan against Mirza Jani Beg of Thatta, who pretended to independence, whereupon the Mirza sent 120 armed *ghrabs* and 200 boats against him. In each of these *ghrabs* there were carpenters for quickly repairing the damages that might be caused by guns. Some of Jani Beg's *ghrabs* were manned by Feringhi soldiers. Jani Beg was eventually defeated, fled, and was pursued till he offered terms, giving up to the imperial general thirty *ghrabs* among other things.[3] In 1574 Akbar

[1] Elliot, vol. i., p. 277.

[2] *Ibid.*, vol. iii., p. 370.

[3] *Ibid.*, vol. i., pp. 247–52, *Tarikh-i-Masumi.*

opened his long-continued campaign against Behar and Bengal, and sent the Khan Khanan Munim Khan with the imperial forces against Daud, who was putting up near Patna and Hajipur. The Emperor determined to personally direct the operations, and embarked with a huge fleet, carrying "all his equipments and establishments, armour, drums, treasure, carpets, kitchen utensils, stud, etc. Two large boats were specially prepared for his own accommodation." When he reached Patna by boat he gave orders for the reduction of the fort of Hajipur, and "Khan Alam was sent off with 3,000 men in boats with the materials required for a siege." After the fall of Hajipur, Daud fled in a boat, and Patna fell into the hands of the Emperor, who appointed Khan Khanan to the government of Bengal, giving him all the boats which he had brought down from Agra, with a large army. But Bengal was not easily pacified. The Mogul jaigirdars in Bengal and Behar attempted to defy Akbar's authority. The Afghans also availed themselves of this opportunity, took up arms, and made themselves masters of Orissa and part of Bengal. Finding that the Afghan and Mogul officers were defiant, Akbar appointed Hindu governors of Bengal, of whom Todar Mall was the first. The second was Raja Man Singh of Jaipur, who ruled Bengal from 1589 to 1604.

It was during Man Singh's viceroyalty that we

find a remarkable outburst of naval activity in Eastern Bengal, and proofs of a naval organization that was being slowly and silently built up by the efforts of some of the independent Hindu landlords of Bengal, while the Mogul Government was busy establishing the Nowwara at Dacca. The chief centres of this Hindu naval activity were Sripur, Bakla or Chandradwipa, in the south-east of the modern district of Backergunj and Chandikan, which is identified with the Saugor Island. The Lord of Sripur was Kedar Roy, who was quite a naval genius but hardly sufficiently known. He had many men-of-war kept always in readiness in his shipyards and naval stations. In 1602 he recovered the island of Sandwipa from the Moguls and placed its government in the hands of the Portuguese under Carvalius. This, however, roused the jealousy and alarm of the King of Arrakan, who forthwith dispatched 150 vessels of war, large and small, to conquer Sandwipa. Kedar Roy, equal to the occasion, at once sent 100 vessels of war in aid of his allies. In the battle that was fought the allies of Kedar Roy came off victorious, and they captured 149 of the enemy's vessels. The King of Arrakan fared equally ill in his second attempt against Kedar Roy's allies, although he dispatched as many as 1,000 war-vessels against them. But Kedar Roy had to face a more powerful enemy in another direction about the same time. For Raja

Man Singh, the then Viceroy of Bengal, was convinced of the necessity of extinguishing the power and independence of Kedar Roy, and sent Manda Roy with 100 war-vessels for the purpose. But in the battle that was fought Manda Roy was slain. This, however, only incited Man Singh to make a second and far stronger attempt to subdue Kedar Roy in A.D. 1604. Kedar Roy, equipped with fully 500 men-of-war, first took the offensive and besieged the Mogul general Kilmak at Srinagara, but was eventually himself taken prisoner after a furious cannonade. He was brought before Man Singh, but soon died of his wounds.[1]

Bakla also was another important centre of naval strength in Bengal under the famous landlord Rāmachandra Roy. His escape with his life from the clutches of Protāpāditya of Jessore, in a boat furnished with guns and propelled by 64 oarsmen, is a well-known fact.[2] The reputation of Rāmachandra as a hero was fully maintained by his son and successor, Kīrtinārāyaṇa, who was

---

[1] *Takmilla-i-Akbarnāma*, in Elliot, vol. vi., pp. 166 ff.

[2] Cf. the following passage from the *Ghatakakārikā*, the Sanskrit chronicle of the period :—

चतुःषष्टिदण्डयुक्ता नौरानीता महामतिः ।
नाविकैः सज्जितास्त्रैः सैन्याद्यैरभिरक्षिता ।

For information regarding Bengali maritime activity of this period I am indebted to Srijukta Nikhilnath Roy's useful work on *Protapaditya* in Bengali.

equally skilful in naval warfare, and succeeded in ousting the Feringhis from their settlements near the mouths of the Meghna. His alliance was courted even by the Nawab of Dacca.

But by far the most important seat of Hindu maritime power of the times in Bengal was that established at Chandikan or Saugor Island by the constructive genius of Protāpāditya, the redoubtable ruler of Jessore. Numbers of men-of-war were always to be found ready for battle and in a seaworthy condition at that naval station. There were also three other places where Protap built his shipyards and dockyards: these were Dudhali, Jāhāja-ghāta, and Chakaśrī, where his ships were built, repaired, and kept.

But the maritime activity of Bengal in this period found its scope not only in war, but also in the gentler arts of peace. Foreign writers and travellers who visited Bengal in the 16th century speak in high terms of the wealth flowing from her brisk sea-borne trade and the greatness and magnificence of some of her ports. Purchas describes Bengal as "plentiful in rice, wheat, sugar, ginger, long-pepper, cotton, and silk, and enjoying also a very wholesome air." Varthema (1503–1508) says of Bengal: "This country abounds more in grain, flesh of every kind, in great quantity of sugar, also of ginger, and of great abundance of cotton, than any country in the world." Ralph Fitch, probably the first English traveller to Bengal (1586), mentions some of the ports and marts of Bengal. One of these was *Tanḍa*, where there was "great trade and traffic of cotton and cotton cloth." Another was *Bacla*, which "is very great and plentiful, and hath store of rice, much cotton cloth, and cloth of silk." The third was *S'ripur* with its "great store of cotton cloth." Of the fourth, viz. *Sonargaon*, he says, "Here is best and finest cloth made of cotton that is in all India. . . . Great store of cotton cloth goeth from here, and much rice, wherewith they serve all India, Ceylon, Pegu, Malacca, Sumatra, and many other places." *Satgaon* was another great emporium of Bengal for foreign commerce, and is thus described by Fitch: "Satgaon is a fair city for a city of the Moors and very plentiful of all things. Here in Bengal they have every day, in one place or other, a great market which they call 'Chandeun,' and they have many great boats which they call 'pencose,' wherewithal they go from place to place and buy rice and many other things; their boats have 24 or 26 oars to row them, they be of great burthen. . . ." Bengal was also noted for her salt trade, the centre of which was Sandwipa, whence "300 ships are yearly laden with salt."

But perhaps the most important commercial centre of Bengal in this period was the city of Gaur, the history of which may be traced as far back as the days of Pala and Sena kings. As the place was surrounded on all sides by rivers it naturally gave a great impetus to boat-building and maritime activity, of which the first proofs we get are in the time of the Pala kings. In the Kalimpur copper-plate inscription of Dharmapaladeva there is a reference to bridges[1] of boats built for the transport of armies, and also to an officer called *Tarik*, who was the general superintendent of boats. In some of the copper-plate inscriptions of the Sena kings, also, there is mention of naval force as an element of their military organization.[2] Under the Musulman kings of Bengal, Gaur continued to grow in prosperity and importance. We have already seen how in the 15th century ambassadors from China to Bengal and from Bengal to China used to carry presents as tokens of mutual friendship between the sovereigns of both the countries.[3] In the 16th century, under the rule of the Hussain Shah dynasty, the city attained its greatest splendour. Hussain Shah (1498–1520 A.D.)

---

[1] स खलु भागीरथीपथप्रवर्त्तमान नानाविधनौवाटकसम्पादितसेतुबन्ध निहित शैलशिखर श्रेणी विभ्रमात्, i.e. "Now from his royal camp of victory, pitched at Pataliputra, where the manifold fleets of boats proceeding on the path of the Bhagirathi make it seem as if a series of mountain-tops had been sunk to build another causeway."—*Ep. Ind.*, vol. iv., 1896–97, p. 249.

[2] नौबलहस्त्यश्व . . .

[3] See p. 197 of this work.

himself maintained a powerful fleet, with which he once invaded Assam.[1] In Hunter's *Statistical Account of Bengal*[2] there is a story related about one Shaikh Bhik of Gaur, a cloth merchant, who once "set sail for Russia with three ships laden with silk cloths, but two of his ships were wrecked somewhere in the neighbourhood of the Persian Gulf." Accounts of the magnificence of the city are given by foreign travellers who visited Bengal about this time. Varthema (1503–1508) mentions how from "the city of Banghella" (Gaur) sail every year "fifty ships laden with cotton and silk stuffs." De Barros gives the following description of the city, based on the accounts of Portuguese travellers who visited it in the reign of Mahmud III. (1532–1538 A.D.): "The chief city of the kingdom is called Gaur. It is said to be three of our leagues in length and contain 200,000 inhabitants. The streets are so thronged with the concourse and traffic of people that they cannot force their way past. A great part of the houses of this city are stately and well-wrought buildings." Manuel de Faria y Souza[3] wrote: "The principal city Gouro, seated on the bank of the Ganges, three leagues in length, containing one million and two hundred

[1] Blochmann's "Koch Bihar and Assam," in the *J.A.S.B.*, 1872, Part i., No. 1.

[2] Vol. vii., p. 95.

[3] *Portuguese Asia*, Stevens, 1698, vol. i., ch. ix., pp. 415 ff.

thousand families, and well fortified; along the streets, which are wide and straight, rows of trees to shade the people, which sometimes in such numbers that some are trod to death." Besides these foreign notices of the prosperity of Gaur we have also some native accounts still extant. We have already made extracts from the account contained in *Kavikaṅkaṇa Chandi* of the adventures of the merchant Dhanapati, who lived many years in Gaur, and of his son S'rīmanta, who sailed in quest of his father to Sinhala in ships of 100 yards length and 20 yards breadth, with prows shaped like Makara, or the head of an elephant or a lion. In one of the old folk-songs of *Gambhirā*,[1] belonging to Malda district, there is an interesting reference to another merchant of the name of Dhanapati, who sailed from Delhi to Gaur in ships that occupied so much of the river that there was scarcely any room left for bathing or taking water.[2] According to Malda local tradition, preserved in some old Bengali MSS., there were several Arab merchants who settled in Gaur for purposes of

---

[1] For an account of these songs, see Mr. Haridāsā Pālit's learned article in the *Journal of the Baṅgīya Sāhitya Parishat*.

[2] গৌড়কিনারা হ্যায় ভাগীরথী নদী
জাহাজসে ছানিয়া হায় ধনপতি।
সব ঘাট বন্ধ কিয়া জাহাজ বোহারাসে
নাহি আদ্‌মি পাবে পাণি ভরনে॥

commerce. One of the MSS. gives a glowing description, through the mouth of Chamban Ali, a merchant from Bagdad, of the port of Gaur as seen from the opposite side of the river, and of the innumerable ships and boats, testifying to the vastness of its maritime trade. Some light is thrown on the growth of the shipbuilding industry of Gaur by an old Bengali MS., a poem, called *Manasāmaṅgalā*, by Jagajjibana. The merchant Chand Saodagar summons to his presence the master-craftsman named Kusai, and orders him to build for him fourteen boats at once. Forthwith goes Kusai with his many apprentices to the forest, where he fells all kinds of trees for materials to build the various parts of the boats with. There were soon hewed out three or four lacs of planks which were afterwards joined together by means of iron nails.[1] It is also a significant fact that some very old masts of ships have been unearthed in some of the villages in the neighbourhood of Pandua through which the Mahānandā once flowed.[2]

---

[1] সাল পিয়াল কাটে খরি তেতলি
কাটিল নিম্বের গাছ গাম্ভারি পারলি।
আম্র কাঠাল কাটে কাটয়ে বকুল
চম্পা খিরনি কাটি করিল নির্মূল॥
. . . . . .
চিরিয়া করিল ফালি লক্ষ তিনি চারি॥

[2] For some of the references given above I am indebted to the courtesy of Mr. Haridāsā Pālit, who has devoted himself to the study of the antiquities of Gaur.

CHAPTER III.

THE MOGUL PERIOD (*continued*): FROM THE REIGN OF AKBAR TO THAT OF AURANGZEB.

WE have now given an account of the development of Indian shipping and shipbuilding in the reign of Akbar and of the contributions made to it not only by his Government but also by private efforts, by independent Hindu and Mahomedan rulers. Nor was this development checked after Akbar's death, but continued through successive reigns.

After the death of Akbar in 1605, Islam Khan, Governor of Bengal, transferred the seat of government from Rajmahal to Dacca, and increased the Nowwara, or fleet, and artillery, which had been established in the time of Akbar in order to check the renewed aggressions of the Afghans and Maggs. As stated in the contemporary Persian account of Shihab-ud-din Talish, "in *Jahangir's reign* the Magg pirates used to come to Dacca for plunder and abduction, and in fact considered the whole of Bengal as their jaigir." [1] Islam Khan shortly afterwards defeated the combined forces of the Rajah of Arrakan and the Portuguese pirate

[1] *J.A.S.B.*, vol. iii., N.S., pp. 424, 425.

Sebastian Gonzales, then in possession of Sandwipa, and commanding an army of 1,000 Portuguese, 2,000 sepoys, 200 cavalry, and 80 well-armed vessels of different sizes, who both made a descent upon the southern part of the province, laying waste the country along the eastern bank of the Megna.

In the *reign of Shah Jahan*, in A.D. 1638, there began a trouble from a new quarter. Even during the closing years of Akbar's reign, the tribes on the eastern frontier of Bengal, belonging to Kuch Behar and Assam, began to cause trouble. In A.D. 1596 an expedition was sent against Lachmi Narayan, the ruler of Kuch Behar, who commanded a large army consisting of 4,000 horse, 200,000 foot, 700 elephants, and a fleet of 1,000 ships (*Akbarnāma*). In 1600 an imperial fleet consisting of 500 ships was sent to encounter the fleet of Parichat, ruler of Kuch Hajo, in the Gujadhar river, who was defeated and taken prisoner (*Padishanāma*). But Baldeo, brother of Parichat, fled to Assam, and having collected an army of Kochis and Assamese, attacked the imperial army, as well as a fleet of nearly 500 ships, and defeated the whole force.[1] At last, in 1638, the Assamese themselves made a hostile descent on Bengal from their boats, sailing down the river Brahmaputra, and had almost reached Dacca when they were met by the Governor of Bengal, Islam Khan Mushedy, with the

[1] *J.A.S.B.*, 1872, Part i., No. 1, pp. 64 ff.

Nowwara. An engagement ensued in which 4,000 of them were slain and fifteen of their boats fell into the hands of the Mogul Government. The Maggs also were continuing their depredations in the southern parts of the district. "The established rental of the country was at this time almost entirely absorbed in jaigirs assigned to protect the coasts from their ravages, and such was the reduced state of the revenues that Fedai Khan obtained the government on condition of paying ten lacs of rupees a year; viz., five lacs to the Emperor and the same sum to Noor Jehan Begum in lieu of the imperial dues; while, on the invasion of the Assamese, it is said that not a single rupee was remitted to Delhi." Matters instead of improving became worse and worse owing to the continued dilapidation of the Bengal fleet on the one hand and the growing power of the Magg and Feringi fleets on the other. When, in A.D. 1639, Prince Shuja was appointed viceroy, "great confusion was caused by his negligence, and the extortion and violence of the clerks (mutasaddis) ruined the pargannahs assigned for maintaining the Nowwarrah (fleet). Many (naval) officers and workmen holding jagir or stipend were overpowered by poverty and starvation."

In the *reign of Aurangzeb*, when Mir Jumla came to Bengal as viceroy in 1660, removing the seat of government again to Dacca, he began "to make a new arrangement of the expenditure and tankhah of the flotilla, which amounted to fourteen lacs of rupees."[1] With a view to guarding against an invasion from Arrakan, Mir Jumla built several forts about the confluence of the Luckia and Issamutty, and constructed several good military roads and bridges in the vicinity of the town.[2] In 1661 Mir Jumla marched against Kuch Behar, and easily annexed the kingdom, when the Raja Bhim Narain fled. In the following year (1662) he embarked on his conquest of Assam with a large force consisting of infantry and artillery and the Nowwara. About 800 hostile ships attacked the imperial fleet, the cannonade lasting the whole night. The Nawab sent Muhammad Munim Beg to assist the fleet. This decided the fate of the engagement, resulting in the capture of 300 or 400 ships of the enemy with a gun on each. The Assamese burnt some 1,000 and odd ships, many of which were large enough to accommodate 80, 70, and 60 sailors, including 123 bachhari ships, like which no other existed in the dockyard at Ghargaon. The imperial fleet used in the engagement consisted of 323 ships, viz.:—

Kosahs	159
Jalbahs	48
Ghrabs	10

[1] MS. Bodleian 598, in *J.A.S.B.*, June, 1907.

[2] Taylor's *Topography and Statistics of Dacca*, p. 76.

Parindahs	7
Bajrahs	4
Patilahs	50
Salbs	2
Patils	1
Bhars	1
Balams	2
Rhatgiris	10
Mahalgiris	5
Palwarahs and other small ships . .	24
Total	323[1]

It was after all a pyrrhic victory, for a terrible sickness spread among the troops, carrying off many naval officers and men, including Mir Jumla himself. At the death of Mir Jumla, the Bengal flotilla was utterly ruined, and, taking advantage of this, the pirates, early in the year 1664, appeared before Dacca, "and defeated Munawwar Khan, Zemindar, who was stationed there with the relics of the Nowwara—a few broken and rotten boats—and bore the high title of Cruising Admiral (*Sardar-i-Sairal*)," and "the few boats that still belonged to the Nowwara were thus lost, and its name alone remained in Bengal." In 1664 Shaista Khan became viceroy; and resolving to suppress piracy at any cost, devoted all his energy to the rebuilding of the flotilla and the creation of a new one. The contemporary Persian manuscript of the Bodleian Library gives some interesting details regarding the

[1] *Fathiyyah-i-ibriyyah*, translated by Blochmann in the *J.A.S.B.*, 1872, Part i., No. 1, pp. 64–96.

means adopted by Shaista Khan to revive the Nowwara. "As timber and shipwrights were required for repairing and fitting out the ships, to every mauza of the province that had timber and carpenters bailiffs were sent with warrants to take them to Dacca." The principal *centres of shipbuilding* at that time appear to have been Hugli, Baleswar, Murang, Chilmari, Jessore and Karibari, where "as many boats were ordered to be built and sent to Dacca as possible." At headquarters, too, Shaista Khan did not for a moment "forget to mature plans for assembling the crew, providing their rations and needments, and collecting the materials for shipbuilding and shipwrights. Hakim Mahammad Hussain, mansabdar, an old, able, learned, trustworthy, and virtuous servant of the Nawab, was appointed head of the shipbuilding department. . . . To all ports of this department expert officers were appointed. Kishore Das, a well-informed and experienced clerk, was appointed to have charge of the pargannahs of the Nowwara and the stipend of the jaigirs assigned to the naval officers and men." As a result of this activity and the ceaseless exertions of the Nawab, we find the magnificent output of as many as 300 ships built in a very short time and equipped with the necessary materials.

To secure bases for the war against the Feringis of Chatgaon, the Nawab posted an officer with 200 ships at Saṅgrāmgara, where the Ganges and the Brahmaputra unite, and another at Dhapa, with 100 ships, to help the former when required. Then the island of Sandwipa was conquered by defeating Dilawwar, a runaway ship-captain of Jahangir's time. At this time a section of the Feringis under their leader, Captain Moor, deserted to the Mogul side. The imperial fleet was placed under Ibn Hussain. It consisted of 288 ships, as described below:—

Ghrabs	21
Salb	3
Kusa	157
Jalba	96
Bachhari	2
Parenda	6
Not specified	3
Total	288

Ibn Hussain advanced with the Nowwara by the sea in co-operation with the army advancing by land, the Nawab himself arranging to supply the expeditionary force constantly with provisions. The first naval battle was fought on a stormy sea. The Arrakanese were put to flight and ten ghrabs captured. The two fleets, with larger ships, again faced each other, and spent the night in distant cannonade. In the morning the imperial fleet advanced towards the enemy, with sails in the first line, then the gharabs, and last the jalbas and kusas side by side. The Arrakanese retreated into the Carnafuli river. The Moguls closed its mouth and then attacked and captured the Arrakanese navy, consisting of 135 ships, viz. :—

Khalu	2
Ghrab	9
Jangi	22
Kusa	12
Jalba	67 (68 ?)
Balam	22

Besides Bengal there were other parts of India in the time of Aurangzeb in which there was a marked development of Indian shipping and maritime commerce. Thomas Bowrey,[1] an English traveller to India during A.D. 1669–1679, has left a very valuable account of countries round the Bay of Bengal, in which are given descriptions and representations of ships and boats, which are "among the best of the kind for this period." The great trading and shipping centre of the time on the Coromandel coast was Metchlepatam (Masulipatam), of which the inhabitants "are great merchant adventurers, and transport vast stocks in the goods aforesaid, both in their own ships as also upon fraught in English ships or vessels." Among the miscellaneous papers at the end of the *Diary* of Strenysham Master there is, pp. 337–339, an

[1] *A Geographical Account of Countries round the Bay of Bengal*, 1669–1675, by Thomas Bowrey, edited by Lieut.-Colonel Sir Richard Carnac Temple, Bart., C.I.E., Series II., vol. xii. (Hakluyt Society publication).

"Account of the trade of Metchlepatam," by Christopher Hotton, dated 9th Jan. 1676–77. He says: "Arriving first in 1657, at which time I found this place in a very flourishing condition, 20 sail of ships of burden *belonging to the native inhabitants* here constantly employed on voyages to Arracan, Pegu, Tanassery, Queda, Malacca, . . . Moca, Persia, and the Maldive Islands."

The King of Golconda also had a mercantile marine. He had several ships "that trade yearly to Arrakan, Tenassery, and Ceylon to purchase elephants for him and his nobility. They bring in some of his ships from fourteen to twenty-five of these vast creatures. They must of necessity be of very considerable burthens and built exceeding strong." Bowrey also saw a ship belonging to the King of Golconda, built for the trade to Mocha in the Red Sea, "which could not be, in my judgment, less than 1,000 tons in burden."[1]

Narsapore, 45 miles north of Masulipatam, was also one of the important shipping centres. It "aboundeth well in timber and conveniences for the building and repairing ships" (p. 99). Morris, in his *Godavari District*, says, "the place was well known more than two centuries ago for its docks for the building and repair of large vessels." In a

---

[1] *A Geographical Account of Countries round the Bay of Bengal*, pp. 72 ff.

"Generall" from Balasor, dated 16 December, 1670, the Factors at the Bay wrote to the Court (*Factory Records, Misc.* no. 3) that they had ordered a ship to be built at "Massapore" in place of the "Madras Pinnace"; they added, "We should ourselves have built another but that neither timber nor workmen are so good as at Massapore."[1]

Madapollum was another shipping centre where "many English merchants and others have their ships and vessels yearly built. Here is the best and well-grown timber in sufficient plenty, the best iron upon the coast; any sort of iron-work is here ingeniously performed by the natives, as spikes, bolts, anchors, and the like. Very expert master-builders there are several here; they build very well, and launch with as much discretion as I have seen in any part of the world. They have an excellent way of making shrouds, stays, or any other rigging for ships."[2]

Bowrey refers to a sort of "ship-money" imposed by Nawab Shaista Khan of Bengal on the mercantile community to build up the naval defence or power of the country. Thus, not satisfied that all, both rich and poor, should bow to him, but wishing the ships upon the water should do the like, the Nawab would every year send down to the mer-

---

[1] *A Geographical Account of Countries round the Bay of Bengal*, pp. 72 ff.

[2] *Ibid.*, pp. 100–5.

chants in Hugli, Jessore, Pipli, and Balasore for a ship or two in each respective place of 400, 500, or 600 tons, to be very well built and fitted, even as if they were to voyage to sea, as also 10, 20, or 30 galleys for to attend them, the Moor's governors having strict orders to see them finished with all speed, and gunned and well manned, and sent up the Ganges as high as Dacca.[1]

Of the Nawab's mercantile marine Bowrey says that it consists of about "20 sail of ships of considerable burden that annually trade to sea from Dacca, Balasore, and Pipli, some to Ceylon, some to Tenessarim. These fetch elephants, and the rest, 6 or 7, yearly go to the Twelve Thousand Islands, called the Maldives, to fetch cowries and cayre (coir), and most commonly do make profitable voyages."[2]

Lastly, Bowrey gives an account of the various kinds of ships and boats that were then built. The *Massoola* boats, used in lading and unlading ships or vessels, "are built very slight, having no timbers in them save 'thafts' to hold their sides together. Their planks are very broad and thin, sewed together with coir; they are flat-bottomed" and most proper for the Coromandel coast; for "all along the shore the sea runneth high and breaketh, to which they do buckle and also to the ground where they

---

[1] *A Geographical Account of Countries round the Bay of Bengal*, pp. 179–80.

[2] *Ibid.*

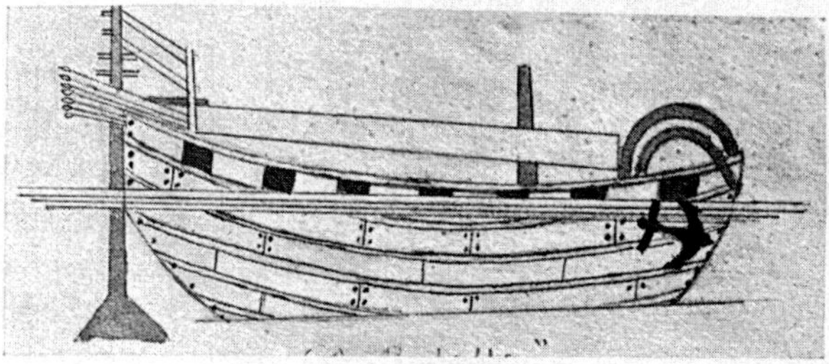

A PATELLA.

AN OLOAKO.

A BUDGAROO.

[*To face p.* 235.

strike."[1] There is another kind of boat called the *catamaran*, made of four, five, or six large pieces of buoyant timber "upon which they can lade three or four tons of weight." In Bengal, Bowrey noticed "great flat-bottomed vessels of an exceeding strength which are called *Patellas* and built very strong. Each of them will bring down 4,000, 5,000, or 6,000 Bengal maunds." Bowrey also mentions several sorts of boats that were in use on rivers. The *Oloako* boats are rowed some with four, some with six oars, and ply for a fare. A *Budgaroo*, a pleasure boat, was used by the upper classes. A *Bajra* was a kind of large boat, fairly clean, the centre of which formed a little room. The *Purgoos* which were seen for the most part between Hugli, Piplo, and Balesore were used for lading and unlading ships. "They will live a long time in the sea, being brought to anchor by the sterne, as their usual way is." *Booras* were "very floaty, light boats, rowing with twenty or thirty oars. These carry salt, pepper, and other goods from Hugli downwards, and some trade to Dacca with salt; they also serve for tow-boats for the ships bound up or down the river." Lastly, there were the "men-of-war prows" which were used in the Malaya Archipelago.[2]

---

[1] *A Geographical Account of Countries round the Bay of Bengal*, p. 43.
[2] *Ibid.*

Dr. Fryer, who visited India about the year 1674, has also left some interesting details about Indian ships and boats. He describes the *Mussoola* as "a boat wherein ten men paddle, the two aftermost of whom are the steersmen, using their paddles instead of rudder: the boat is not strengthened with knee-timber, as ours are; the bended planks are sewed together with rope-yarn of the cocoe and caulked with dammar (a sort of rosin taken out of the sea) so artificially that it yields to every ambitious surf." [1] He describes catamarans as formed of "logs lashed to that advantage that they waft all their goods, only having a sail in their midst, and paddles to guide them." Dr. Fryer was landed at Masulipatam by one of the country boats, which he describes as being "as large as one of our ware-barges and almost of that mould, sailing with one sail like them, but paddling with paddles instead of spreads, and carry a great burden with little trouble; out-living either ship or English skiff over the bar."

On the west coast also there were important

---

[1] *Early Records of British India*, by J. T. Wheeler, p. 54. Major H. Bevan in his *Thirty Years in India* (1808–1838), p. 14, vol. i., speaks of the Masula boat as "admirably contrived to resist the impetus of the surf in the roadstead of Madras. It is built of planks of wood sewed together with *sun*, a species of twine, and caulked with coarse grass, not a particle of iron being used in the entire construction. Both ends are sharp, narrow, and tapering to a point so as easily to penetrate the surf." Bevan also remarks, "The build of the boats all along the coast of India varies according to the localities for which they are destined, and each is peculiarly adapted to the nature of the coast on which it is used."

A PURGOO.

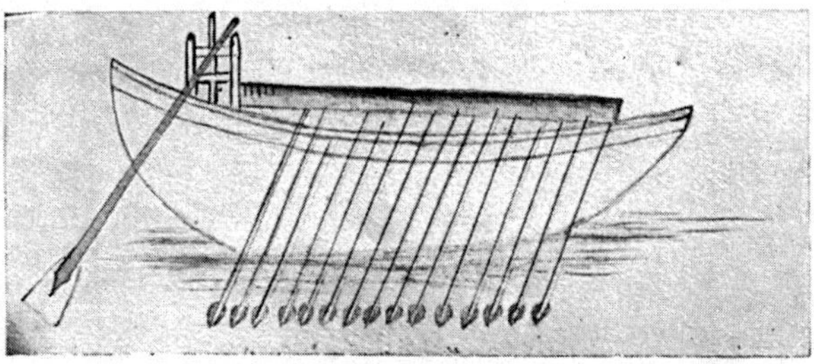

A BOORA.

MAN-OF-WAR PROW.

[*To face p.* 236.

shipping centres in Aurangzeb's time. According to Dr. Fryer (1672) Aurangzeb had at Surat four great ships always in pay to carry pilgrims to Mecca free of cost. These vessels were "huge, unshapen things." He also noticed at Surat some Indian ships or merchantmen carrying thirty or forty pieces of cannon, and "three or four men-of-war as big as third-rate ships, " as also frigates fit to row or sail, made with prows instead of beaks, more useful in rivers and creeks than in the main." The captain of a ship was called *Nacquedah* (Pers. *nakhuda*, ship-master) and the boatswain *Tindal*. Some of the larger Indian ships at Surat, of which the names are also known, fell a prey to the pirates that infested the whole of the western coast, and became a terrible scourge to the Indian trade in the time of the Emperor Aurangzeb, just as their brethren on the west coast, the Magg and Feringhi pirates, were harrying deltaic Bengal. Thus in August, 1691, a ship belonging to Abdul Guffoor, who was the wealthiest and most influential merchant in Surat, was captured by pirates at the mouth of the Surat river with nine lacs in hard cash on board. Soon afterwards another ship, named *Futteh Mahmood*, with a valuable cargo, also belonging to Abdul Guffoor, was similarly seized by an Englishman called Every, who was the most notorious pirate of the time. A few days after the capture of the *Futteh Mahmood*, Every took off Sanjan, north of

Bombay, a ship belonging to the Emperor Aurangzeb himself, called the *Gunj Suwaie* ("exceeding treasure"). According to Khafi Khan, the historian, the *Gunj Suwaie* was the largest ship belonging to the port of Surat. She carried eight guns and four hundred matchlocks, and was deemed so strong that she disdained the help of a convoy. She was annually sent to Mecca, carrying Indian goods to Mocha and Jedda. She was returning to Surat with the result of the season's trading, amounting to fifty-two lacs of rupees in silver and gold, with Ibrahim Khan as her captain, and when she had come within eight or nine days from Surat she was attacked and seized by the English pirate "sailing in a ship of much smaller size, and nothing a third or fourth of the armament." Another capture of Every was the *Rampura*, a Cambay ship with a cargo valued at Rs.1,70,000. Shivaji also, as we shall presently see, used to intercept these Mogul ships plying between Surat and Mecca by means of the fleet which he fitted out at his ports built on the coasts.[1]

During the same period a great impetus to Indian shipping and maritime enterprise was given by the great Mahratta leader, S'ivaji,[2] who liberally

---

[1] *Early Records of British India*, by J. T. Wheeler; *The Pirates of Malabar*, by Colonel J. Biddulph.

[2] Cf. Duff's *History of the Mahrattas*, p. 85: "Having seen the advantage . . . . derived from a fleet S'ivaji used great exertions to fit out a marine. He rebuilt or strengthened Kolaba, repaired Severndroog

patronized the shipbuilding industry. The growth of the Mahratta power was accompanied by the formation of a formidable fleet. Several docks were built, such as those in the harbours of Vijayadoorga, Kolaba, Sindhuvarga, Ratnagiri, Anjanvela, and the like, where men-of-war were constructed.[1] In 1698, Conajee Angria succeeded to the command of the Mahratta navy with the title of Darya-Saranga. The career of Angria was one long series of naval exploits and achievements rare in the annals of Indian maritime activity, but unfortunately "dismissed in a few words by our Indian historians."[2] Under him the Mahratta naval power reached its high-water mark. Bombay had to wage a long half-century of amateur warfare to subdue the Angrian power. It would be tedious to relate all the details of their long-continued conflict, but we may mention some of the more important events. In the name of the Satara chief, Angria was master of the whole

---

and Viziadroog, and prepared vessels at all these places. His principal depot was the harbour of Kolaba, twenty miles south of Bombay." Also, "History of the Konkan" in the *Bombay Gazetteer*, vol. i., Part ii., pp. 68 foll.: "Shivaji caused a survey to be made of the coast, and having fixed on Malvan as the best protection for his vessels and the likeliest place for a stronghold, he built forts there, rebuilt and strengthened Suvarndurg, Ratnagiri, Jaygad, Anjanabel, Vijiaydurg, and Kolaba, and prepared vessels at all these places."

[1] Cf. Duff's *History of the Mahrattas*, pp. 172: "The Mahrattas continued in possession of most of their forts on the coast; they had maritime depots at Severndroog and Viziadroog, but the principal rendezvous of their fleet continued, as in the time of Shivaji, at Kolaba."

[2] Col. Biddulph in *The Pirates of Malabar*.

coast from Bombay to Vingorla, and, with a fleet of armed vessels carrying thirty and forty guns apiece, he soon became a menace to the European trade of the west coast. In 1707 his ship attacked the *Bombay* frigate, which was blown up after a brief engagement. In 1710 he seized and fortified Kanhery, and his ships fought the *Godolphin* for two days. In 1712 he captured the Governor of Bombay's armed yacht, and fought two East Indiamen bound for Bombay. In 1716 he made prize of four private ships from Mahim, an East Indiaman named *Success*, and a Bengal ship named *Otter*. Then followed, successively, expeditions against Gheriah, Kanhery, and Colaba, which all proved abortive and ineffectual against the power of the Angrian fleet. In 1729 Conajee Angria died, and was succeeded at Severndoorg by Sambhuji Angria, who carried on his predatory policy for nearly thirty years. In 1730 the Angrian squadron of four grabs and fifteen gallivats destroyed the galleys *Bombay* and *Bengal* off Colaba. In 1732, five grabs and three gallivats attacked the East Indiaman *Ockham*. In 1735 a valuable East Indiaman named the *Derby*, with a great cargo of naval stores, fell into Sambhuji's hands. In 1738 a Dutch squadron of seven ships-of-war and seven sloops was repulsed from Gherriah. In 1740 some fifteen sail of Angria's fleet gave battle to four ships returning from China. The same year Sambhuji attacked Colaba with his army and forty or fifty gallivats, but was opposed by the English. In 1743 Sambhuji died, leaving his predatory policy to be continued by his successor, Toolaji. His greatest success was achieved in 1749, when Toolaji's fleet of five grabs and a swarm of gallivats surrounded and cannonaded the *Restoration*, the most efficient ship of the Bombay Marine. "Toolajee had now become very powerful. From Cutch to Cochin his vessels swept the coast in greater numbers than Conajee had ever shown. The superior sailing powers of the Mahratta vessels enabled them to keep out of range of the big guns, while they snatched prizes within sight of the men-of-war." In 1754 the Dutch suffered a severe loss at Toolaji's hands, losing a vessel loaded with ammunition, and two large ships. The next year the English and Peshwa formed an alliance against him, and jointly attacked Severndoorg, which was reduced after forty-eight hours' fighting. Then followed the well-planned expedition led by Admiral Watson and Clive against Gherriah, resulting in the burning of the Angrian fleet, consisting of "three three-masted ships carrying twenty guns each, nine two-masted carrying from twelve to sixteen guns, thirteen gallivats carrying from six to ten guns, thirty others unclassed, two on the stocks, one of them pierced for forty guns." The following is a very interesting description by an *eye-witness* of Angria's fleet: "His fleet consisted of grabs and gallivats. . . . The grabs have rarely more than two masts. . . . They are very broad in proportion to their length. . . . On the main deck under the forecastle are mounted two pieces of cannon of nine or twelve pounders, which point forwards through the portholes cut in the bulkhead and fire over the prow; the cannon of the broadside are from six to nine pounders. The gallivats are large row-boats rarely exceeding seventy tons. The gallivats are covered with a spar deck, made for lightness of split bamboos, and these only carry pettera roes, which are fixed on swivels in the gunnel of the vessel: but those of the largest size have a fixed deck on which they mount six or eight pieces of cannon, from two to four pounders. They have forty or fifty stout oars, and may be rowed four miles an hour. Eight or ten grabs and forty or fifty gallivats, crowded with men, generally composed Angria's principal fleet, destined to attack ships of force or burthen."[1] The fall of Gherriah meant the extinction of Mahratta naval power, which had been the terror of the coast for a whole half-century.

---

[1] *Bombay Gazetteer*, vol. i., Part ii., p. 89.

"MAHRATTA GRABS AND GALLIVATS ATTACKING AN ENGLISH SHIP."

(From the picture in the possession of Sir Ernest Robinson.)

[*To face p.* 242.

CHAPTER IV.

LATER TIMES.

WITH the rise of the British power following upon the decline of the Mogul Empire after Aurangzeb, Indian shipping naturally received a great impetus at the hands of Englishmen. It appears to be quite forgotten that for nearly two centuries and a half British India maintained a navy of respectable size and of admirable efficiency. This navy has behind it an interesting and inspiring record of many brilliant achievements and much solid and useful work, especially in marine surveying. Colonel the Hon. Leicester Stanhope, in 1827, said: "Never was there an instance of any ship of the Bombay Marine (as it was then named) having lowered her flag to an enemy of equal force." The history began in 1613, when a squadron was formed at Surat to afford protection from the aggressions of the Portuguese and of the pirates who infested the Indian seas. The naval establishment was put on a permanent footing in 1615, and it attained respectable dimensions by the second half of the 17th century. In 1669 the Court of Directors appointed Mr. W. Pett as their shipbuilder at Bombay, whither the establishment was previously removed. It was then designated as the Bombay Marine. A building-yard was maintained at Surat till 1735, when most of the work was transferred to Bombay, where the establishment had been greatly enlarged. This was the beginning of the association of the eminent Parsi shipbuilders with the Indian and Imperial Navy services. Lowjee Nassaranjee, the foreman of Surat shipyard, followed the establishment from Surat to Bombay. The history of this dockyard is that of the rise of a talented Parsi family. The size of the yard was increased in 1757. In 1771 Lowjee introduced into it his two grandsons, Framjee Manseckjee and Jamsetjee Bomenjee. In 1774 Lowjee died, succeeded by these two worthy followers, who soon built two ships of 900 tons. It was under the supervision of these talented Parsi shipbuilders that, in this yard, besides those for the Bombay Marine, there were built in the latter part of the 18th and earlier part of the 19th century for the Royal Navy nine ships of the line, seven frigates, and six smaller vessels. Thus, "in 1802, the Admiralty ordered men-of-war for the King's Navy to be constructed at this spot. They intended to have sent out a European builder, but the merits of Jumsetjee being made known to their lordships, they ordered him to continue as master-builder." The excellent construction of two frigates and a line-of-battle ship spread the fame of this worthy Parsi over England. The under-mentioned Parsis held successively the appointment of head builders in the Bombay Government Dockyard from 1736 up to 1837:—

From 1736 to 1774	. . .	Lowjee
" 1774 " 1783	. . .	Manseckjee and Bomenjee
" 1793 " 1805	. . .	Framjee and Jamsetjee
" 1805 " 1811	. . .	Jamsetjee and Ruttonjee
" 1811 " 1821	. . .	Jamsetjee and Nowrojee
" 1821 " 1837	. . .	Nowrojee and Cursetjee

The degree of efficiency which this dockyard reached under these Parsi shipbuilders will be also evident from the statement of a visitor, who, describing Bombay in 1775, said: "Here is a dockyard, large and well-contrived, with all kinds of naval stores deposited in proper warehouses: and . . . forges for making anchors. It boasts such a dry dock as is, perhaps, not to be seen in any part of Europe, either for size or convenient situation."[1]

Lieut.-Col. A. Walker[2] thus wrote in 1811 of the Bombay docks and Bombay-built ships:—"The docks that have recently been constructed at Bombay are capable of containing vessels of any force. Bombay is our grand naval arsenal in

---

[1] *The History of the Indian Navy*, in two volumes, by Lieutenant C. R. Low, I.N.; *Bombay Times*, 18th May, 1839; *Papers relating to Shipbuilding in India*, by John Phipps (1840), late of the Master Attendant Office; Sir Cyprian Bridge on "India and the Navy," in the London *Spectator* of April 9th, 1910.

[2] *Considerations on the Affairs of India*, written in the year 1811 (445—vi., p. 316).

India." Bombay was possessed of great natural facilities for the construction of ships, for, "situated as she is between the forests of Malabar and Gujarat, she receives supplies of timber with every wind that blows." Besides, the teak-wood vessels of Bombay were greatly superior to the oaken walls of Old England. Lieut.-Col. A. Walker wrote, in 1811: "It is calculated that every ship in the Navy of Great Britain is renewed every twelve years. It is well known that teak-wood built ships last fifty years and upwards.[1] Many ships Bombay-built after running fourteen or fifteen years have been brought into the Navy and were considered as strong as ever. The *Sir Edward Hughes* performed, I believe, eight voyages as an Indiaman before she was purchased for the Navy. No Europe-built Indiaman is capable of going more than six voyages with safety." But Bombay-built ships were superior to those built elsewhere not only in point of durability but also in that of cheapness. "Ships built at Bombay," observes

[1] The late Sister Nivēditā related to me the interesting and significant but hardly known fact that such of our old wooden ships as still survive (for the seasoned wood of which our ships are built has a definite length of life) have passed at second and third hand into the coast trade of North-western Europe, and are still to be met with in Norway, Scotland, Holland, and other little countries on the seaboard. And so the good old sail shipping which steam shipping has weeded out from everywhere else in the world, still lingers on in India, and to her is given the chance of reviving it and giving it back to a world which cannot outgrow its need.

the same writer, "also are executed by one-fourth cheaper than in the docks of England, so that the English-built ships requiring to be renewed every twelve years, the expense is quadruple."

The East India Company also helped to build up the Bengal Marine, thus continuing, in a sense, the work of the Mogul Emperor in connection with the Nowwara. But a very calamitous event led them to revive shipbuilding in Bengal: it was the famine produced in the Carnatic by Hyder Ali's invasion in 1780, which necessitated the transport of grain from Bengal to the English settlements on the Coromandel coast. The first efforts in shipbuilding were made in districts like Sylhet, Chittagong, and Dacca. Mr. Lindsay, Collector of Sylhet in 1780, had one ship built of 400 tons burden, and also a fleet of twenty ships, which he sent to Madras loaded with rice on the occasion of the famine.[1] But Calcutta soon became the centre of regular shipbuilding. The earliest specimens of regular Calcutta-built ships were produced in the year 1781. From 1781 to 1800 inclusive, thirty-five ships, with a total tonnage of 17,020, were built on the Hugli, chiefly at Calcutta; in 1801, nineteen ships were built, of 10,079 tons; in 1813, twenty-one ships, 10,376 tons. Including the above, from 1801 to 1821 both inclusive, there were built on the

[1] *Assam District Gazetteer*, vol. ii. (Sylhet), p. 155.

Hugli 237 ships, of 105,693 tons, which, reckoned at an average cost of 200 rupees per ton, makes the enormous sum of two crores of rupees and upwards; a considerable part of which sum was absorbed in the *payment of wages to native artificers and labourers*, to the great benefit of the country.[1]

The first dry dock constructed at Calcutta was a small one at the Bankshall in 1790 for the Government pilot vessels; subsequent to which several large docks were constructed at Howrah and Sulkea; in 1803 the Kidderpore dock was founded by Mr. W. Waddell, the Company's first master-builder, who was succeeded by J. and R. Kyd, and who for nearly thirty years built and repaired all the Company's Bengal vessels and constructed a great many fine ships, twenty-four in number, and vessels for individuals.[2]

About the materials of which the Bengal ships were constructed, Antony Lambert thus wrote in 1802: They consist of teak timber and planks, imported from Pegu; *saul* and *sisoo* timber from Behar, Oudh, and the inexhaustible forests that skirt the hills which form the northern boundaries of Bengal and Behar. The ribs, knees, and breast-hooks or "the frame of the ship," are composed

---

[1] *Papers Relating to Shipbuilding in India*, by John Phipps, Introduction.

[2] *Ibid.*

generally of *sisoo* timber, the beams and inside planks of *saul*, and the bottoms, sides, decks, keels, sternposts, etc., of teak. The excellence of teak for the purpose of shipbuilding and its durability are too well known to require any description, although Pegu teak is not reckoned equal to what grows on the Malabar coast and near Surat. Of *sisoo* and *saul* timber, the former is admirably adapted to shipbuilding from its size, form, and firm texture, and as it produces crooked timbers and knees of every shape and dimension for vessels of full forms and of any magnitude, even for a ship-of-war of the first rate; and that of the latter furnishes excellent beams, knees, and inside planks.

Lord Wellesley, the Governor-General of India, was able, in 1800, to thus testify to the growth and possibilities of Calcutta as a shipping centre :—

> The port of Calcutta contains about 10,000 tons of shipping, built in India, of a description calculated for the conveyance of cargoes. From the quantity of private tonnage now at command in the port of Calcutta, from the state of perfection which the art of shipbuilding has already attained in Bengal (promising a still more rapid progress and supported by abundant and increasing supply of timbers), it is certain that this port will always be able to furnish tonnage to whatever extent may be required for conveying to the Port of London the trade of the private British merchants of Bengal.

From a "Register of Ships built on the Hugli from 1781–1839 (including Calcutta, Howrah, Sulkea, Cosipore, Tittaghar, Kidderpore, and Fort Gloucester)," it appears that the total number of ships built was 376. The greatest building years were 1801, 1813, and 1876, when 10,079, 10,376, and 8,198 tons respectively were put in.

The Indian Navy, which was thus created and built up by the efforts of the East India Company, took an active part in the first and second Burmese wars and the first China war. A great deal of its service was performed outside local Indian waters, in the Persian Gulf, in the Red Sea, and on the shores of East Africa. It also protected and facilitated the trading operations of Indian merchants with distant ports.

The decline of the Indian Marine began after 1840, no large ships having been built after that date. It was finally abolished in April, 1863, shortly after the assumption of the Government of India by the Crown.

A very interesting account, together with very fine sketches of the typical Indian (Hindu) ships that were in use in the earlier part of the 19th century, is given by a Frenchman, F. Baltazar Solvyns (1811) in his *Les Hindous*[1] (tome troisième). In his introduction to this work he remarks :—

> In ancient times the Indians excelled in the art of constructing vessels, and the present Hindus can in this respect still offer models to Europe—

---

[1] This rare work is to be found in the splendid library of Mr. Abanindranath Tagore, the renowned Bengali artist, to whom I also owe the reproductions from the Sculptures of Borobudur. The French reprint was issued 1808–12; there is an earlier reprint published by Orme, London, 1804, but neither is complete. The original folio edition of 1799 has 250 coloured plates.

so much so that the English, attentive to everything which relates to naval architecture, have borrowed from the Hindus many improvements which they have adopted with success to their own shipping. . . . The Indian vessels unite elegance and utility, and are models of patience and fine workmanship.

He has described some of the typical Indian vessels. A *Pinnace* or *Yacht* was a strongly masted ship, divided into two or three apartments, one for company, another for the beds, and a third as a cabinet, besides a place called *varandah* forwards for the servants. Ballasor, the principal entrance of the Hugli, is described as being frequented by different sorts of vessels, and particularly by large ships from Bombay, Surat, and other parts of the western coast. The vessels from the Ganges were called *Schooners*, which were very well fitted out and "able to make a voyage to Europe," their pilots being "very skilful." The *Grab* was a ship with three masts, a pointed prow, and a bowsprit; its crew consisting of a Nicodar or captain and a few clashies or Moorish sailors. The grabs were built at Bombay, their pointed prow signifying Hindu construction. The *Bangles* were the largest Indian boats, some of them carrying four thousand or five thousand maunds of rice. *Brigs* were ships that came from the coast of Coromandel and Malabar, bringing to Calcutta the produce of those countries. To the coast of Coromandel also belonged the *Dony*, with one mast, resembling a sloop. Its deck consisted of a few planks fastened on each side. It was badly rigged. *Pattooas*, lastly, were those ships that differed from other vessels by their being clincher-built; "the boards are one upon the other, fastened by little pieces of iron in the form of cramps. The yard is always without sail, and the sails are hoisted and lowered by blocks."

PINNACE.

[*To face p.* 252.

BANGLES.

[*To face p.* 252.

GRAB.

[To face p. 252.

PATTOOA.

[To face p. 252.

DONY.

[*To face p.* 252.

BRICK.

[*To face p.* 252.

VIEW OF BALLASORE ROADS.

[To face p. 252.

CONCLUSION.

THUS has passed away one of the great national industries of India after a long and brilliant history, covering, as we have seen, a period of more than twenty centuries. It was undoubtedly one of the triumphs of Indian civilization, the chief means by which that civilization asserted itself and influenced other alien civilizations. India now is without this most important organ of national life. There can hardly be conceived a more serious obstacle in the path of her industrial development than this almost complete extinction of her shipping and shipbuilding. And yet India certainly is one of the countries which can ill spare a national, indigenous shipping. The sea-borne trade of India is continually expanding, with the result of increasing our dependence on foreign shipping, and for this we have, on a rough estimate, to pay a price of about 25 crores of rupees a year. We have trade relations with every quarter of the globe, not only with the Asiatic mainland but also with Europe and Africa on one side and Australasia and America on the other.

The total value of this trade is about 344·2 crores of rupees, that of imports being 161·8 crores and exports 182·3 crores, and the entire trade lies at the mercy of foreign shippers, who are at liberty to impose on us whatever freights they wish to charge for the use of their ships. Even in the matter of our coastal or inter-portal trade, which is also expanding, aggregating in value about 46·37 crores of rupees, a policy of free trade is pursued, throwing it open to the shipping of all the world, instead of reserving it, as almost all other countries do, for the national shipping, so that about 85 per cent. is appropriated by foreign shipping, leaving only one-seventh to the native. Similarly our entire passenger traffic is in the hands of foreign shippers: our Mahomedan pilgrims to Mecca and other places; our emigrants and immigrants, numbering on an average more than 25,000 per year; our passengers that voyage within Indian limits, numbering over 15 lacs every year; and, lastly, the outgoing and relieving British soldiers of the Indian Army, numbering more than 25,000 every year, their transport costing annually about 55½ lacs of rupees—all these have to voyage in foreign ships, while even in the matter of the conveyance of mails there is no Indian steamship company that can take up the work and appropriate the yearly postal subsidy of 7·8 lacs of rupees that now goes to a foreign company. The extent of our dependence will be evident from the fact that in the oceanic trade, of which the total tonnage is 11,800,000 tons, our indigenous shipping represents only 95,000 tons, or only about ·8 per cent.; while of the aggregate tonnage of 29·61 million tons in the inter-portal trade, only 3·24 million tons is our own, and over 89 per cent. foreign. Our national shipping at the present day means only 130 vessels of under 80 tons each, used in the oceanic trade, and 7,280 in the inter-portal trade of the country of under 20 tons each, making up in all the insignificant number of 7,410 vessels, large and small, for a country, or rather a continent, whose seaboard extends over a length of 4,000 miles and upwards. Our shipbuilding now is so contracted as to give employment to only 14,321 men, who build only about 125 galbats a year in shipyards, of which the number is now reduced to only 48, while the aggregate capital yearly invested in shipbuilding may be estimated at between 5 and 6 lacs of rupees.

It goes without saying that in the present state of things it is idle to expect that Indian industry and commerce can advance by leaps and bounds, handicapped as they are by the want of a fully developed Indian shipping. It therefore behoves Government and all who are interested in the material progress of India to be fully alive to the importance and necessity of reviving and restoring on modern lines a lost industry that rendered such a brilliant service in the past, and with which are so vitally bound up the prospects of Indian economic advancement.

INDEX I.—SUBJECTS.

A

B

D

E

F

INDEX I.—SUBJECTS

N

O

P

INDEX II.—PROPER NAMES.

INDEX II.—PROPER NAMES

INDEX II.—PROPER NAMES

INDEX II.—PROPER NAMES

R

T